Thomas Jefferson's Architectural Drawings

Thomas Jefferson
Pencil portrait by [William Russell Birch] copied from the "medallion portrait"
painted from life by Gilbert Stuart in 1805.

Thomas Jefferson's Architectural Drawings

Compiled and with Commentary and a Check List

By FREDERICK DOVETON NICHOLS

Charlottesville: Thomas Jefferson Foundation, Inc.

In memory of Frederick Doveton Nichols (1911-1995), gentleman and scholar

Copyright © 1961, 1995, 2008 *Thomas Jefferson Foundation, Inc.*

First Edition 1960 · *Second Edition* 1971 · *Third Edition* 1975 · *Fourth Edition* 1978

Second Printing 1984 · *Third Printing* 1988 · *Fourth Printing* 1995 · *Fifth Printing* 2001 · *Sixth Printing* 2008

The Thomas Jefferson Foundation and The University Press of Virginia wish to ac-
knowledge the generosity of the Massachusetts Historical Society in making avail-
able its 1960 PICTURE BOOK for republication in this revised edition.

MONTICELLO™

The front elevation of Monticello, in Jefferson's first version, is reproduced on the cover (see 48).

Linotype Monticello, a type face specially designed for *The Papers of Thomas Jefferson*,
has been used for the text of this publication.

This reprint was made possible by the Martin and Luella Davis Publications Endowment.

ISBN: 0-8139-0328-9

Library of Congress Catalog Card Number: 78-150354

Composition by The Anthoensen Press, Portland, Maine

Printed by The Stinehour Press, Lunenburg, Vermont

FOREWORD
Thomas Jefferson's Architectural Development

ARCHITECTURE first captured Thomas Jefferson's imagination while he was a student in Williamsburg, when he bought his first architectural book from an old cabinetmaker near the William and Mary college gate. "Architecture is my delight," he was quoted as saying in later years, "and putting up, and pulling down, one of my favorite amusements."

But the buildings of Williamsburg were not all to his liking. As he wrote in 1781-1782 in *Notes on Virginia*, "The Capitol is a light and airy structure, with a portico in front of two orders," "The Palace is not handsome without, but it is spacious and commodious within, is prettily situated, and with the grounds annexed to it, is capable of being made an elegant seat." For the college and hospital he had only contempt: they "are rude, mis-shapen piles, which, but that they have roofs, would be taken for brick-kilns." He found the houses of Williamsburg inferior to those of Annapolis (he even measured the superb Harwood-Hammond house) but preferred the gardens of the Virginia town. He lamented the fact that "a workman could scarcely be found here capable of drawing an order. The genius of architecture seems to have shed its maledictions over this land." But he did not despair: "Architecture being one of the fine arts, and as such within the department of a professor of the college . . . perhaps a spark may fall on some young subjects of natural taste, kindle up their genius, and produce a reformation in this elegant and useful art." Before he wrote this, he had made plans for redesigning the Palace and the college.

Jefferson was only twenty-four when he began the design of Monticello, and until he died it was never really out of his thoughts. "All my wishes end," he wrote in 1787, "where I hope my days will end, at Monticello." Like many English gentlemen, Jefferson was a disciple of Palladio, regarding the great sixteenth-century Italian architect as the ultimate authority. Palladio had recommended building on an elevated site, and by the mid-eighteenth century mountain pinnacles and crags were becoming fashionable in romantic literature. But perhaps the splendid views from Monticello enchanted Jefferson. He wrote years later to his beautiful friend, Maria Cosway, describing his mountain top "where nature has spread so rich a mantle under the eye. How sublime to look down into the workhouse of nature, to see her clouds, hail, snow, thunder, all fabricated at our feet! and the glorious sun when rising as if out of a distant water, just gilding the tops of the mountains and giving life to all nature." His idea for a classical villa on a mountain top was highly original: even in England only garden towers and temples were built on such eminences.

As early as 1767 Jefferson began studies for Monticello. There are notes and calculations for it at the back of his oldest pocket account book for that year. Until 1770 he was busy with preliminary studies of the plan and elevation of the mansion, using James Gibbs's *Rules for Drawing the Several Parts of Architecture* and *Book of Architecture*, Robert Morris' *Select Architecture*, and Palladio's *Four Books of Architecture* (Leoni's edition of 1715 or 1742, or both).

His first idea was for a house with a center block and flanking wings. The source seems to have been *Select Architecture*, as one of the oldest drawings extant for Monticello is a tracing he made of Plate 3. Jefferson then experimented in wood and in brick, with a two-story portico and an arcaded first floor, a motif reappearing in 1817 at the University of Virginia in Pavilion VII. It was to become a favorite Virginia house plan, antedating the James Semple house in Williamsburg, which has a similar plan. Jefferson's version (No. 1 and Cover) was of the same type, and after the basement walls were up, he added the octagonal bays to the parlor and the ends of the building (No. 4 and Cover).

Meanwhile work had begun on the first "outchamber" in the autumn of 1769. It is the southwest outbuilding, and the dimensions for it are in the account book of 1767. The stone house was probably begun at this time on Mulberry Row (No. 17). In the summer of 1770 the outchamber was plastered, and on November 26 Jefferson "Moved to Monticello." The following February, in one of the first dated letters from there, he wrote: "I have lately removed to the mountain from whence this is dated. . . . I have here but one room, which, like the cobbler's serves me for parlour for kitchen and hall. I may add, for bedchamber and study too. . . . I have hope, however, of getting more elbow room this summer." He was to need it, for on New Year's Day of 1772 he married. He now decided to suppress the wings of his house in order to retain the fine views (No. 2), and he was thoroughly happy developing his building plans and making time studies amazingly similar to those of modern industry. Throughout the Revolution he pushed the work, and finally, in 1782, the first version of the house was almost finished (No. 4 and Cover). According to the Chevalier de Chastellux it consisted of "one large square pavilion, the entrance of which is by two porticoes, ornamented with pillars." But the Jeffersons were not to enjoy it for long, for on September 6 Martha Jefferson died, leaving her husband disconsolate.

While at work on Monticello, he had made plans also for buildings at Williamsburg and Richmond. No. 9 shows a plan for an octagonal chapel. The notes for it are headed "Design of a Chapel, the model of the temple of Vesta. Pallad. B. 4. Pl. 38. 39." It probably dates from about 1770, from the evidence of the watermarks, and seems to have been designed for erection at Williamsburg. It was also based upon *Select Architecture*, Plate 31, "of an octagonal Temple or Chapel, 60 Feet in outer Diameter and the internal 40 Feet."

No. 10 shows his "Plan for an addition to the College of William and Mary, drawn at the request of Ld. Dunmore." It dates probably from 1771 or 1772, and the palace court arrangement seems to have been suggested by Palladio's Palazzo Thiene at Vicenza, Book II, Plate 9, which shows such an enclosed court. Only the foundations for this addition were ever completed.

Nos. 7 and 8 represent Jefferson's ideas for remodeling the Governor's Palace in Williamsburg. Drawn apparently between 1772 and 1781, one is for measurements, and the other, showing changes, also provides for a temple form house with two porticoes. Although he also

seems to have made studies for replacing the Palace with a *villa rotonda*, based upon Palladio's Villa at Vicenza, Book II, Plates 14 and 15, he did not pursue the idea. His prophetic idea for a temple form building, the first in the modern world (with the exception of the small garden temples in England) is a striking example of Jefferson's leadership as one of the innovators of the movement of Romantic Classicism.

In 1776 Jefferson had presented to the House of Delegates a bill for the design of the new capital in Richmond. It was a revolutionary bill which, for the first time, provided separate buildings to house the various branches of the new government. In 1780 it was decided to erect the public buildings, and Jefferson was appointed head of a committee for this purpose. He then drew up plans for enlarging the town with some four hundred new lots, located four to a block, on a gridiron plan (No. 33). Later he believed that yellow fever and other diseases could be prevented by "building our cities on a more open plan. Take, for instance, the chequerboard for a plan. Let the black squares only be building squares, and the white ones be left open, in turf and trees. Every square of houses will be surrounded by four open squares, and every house will front an open square. . . . The plan of the town . . . will be found handsome and pleasant." He also made studies for the Halls of Justice and then began his studies for the Richmond Capitol, as two large plans in the Huntington Library indicate. While the interior was not so formally arranged as it was in the later designs (No. 12), they prove that he had arrived at the conception of a temple form building before he left America and long before he met Clérisseau in France, the architect who helped him with the final design and with the model. Excepting his studies for the Governor's Palace, this idea was entirely new and was not to be used in Europe for a monumental building until the Madeleine was started in Paris in 1807.

Thus both in Williamsburg and in Richmond, before he went abroad in 1784, Jefferson had projected designs for buildings which by "introducing into the State an example of architecture in the classic style of antiquity," as he wrote in his Autobiography, would improve the status of the arts in Virginia. The earlier designs for the Capitol showed a rectangular temple form, with Ionic porticoes and eight columns at either end. Apparently porticoes were also intended for the Halls of Justice. In Nos. 11 and 13 the design is more typically Roman, with only one portico. Some details, drawn in a more professional hand than Jefferson's, indicate that Clérisseau's only changes were in the doors and windows and in the panels over them. The French architect also suggested lowering the pitch of the pediment. Jefferson had followed the proportions of Palladio in his detailing, but the model indicates that the window details were changed to conform to those of the Maison Carrée, as drawn by Clérisseau.

According to Jefferson, "the Maison Quarée of Nismes, an ancient Roman temple, being considered as the most perfect model existing of what may be called Cubic architecture, I applied to M. Clérisseault . . . to have me a model of the building made in stucco, only changing the order from Corinthian to Ionic, on account of the difficulty of the Corinthian capitals. . . . To adapt the exterior to our use, I drew a plan for the interior, with the apartments necessary for legislative, executive, and judiciary purposes. . . . These were forwarded to the directors in 1786, and were carried into execution."

Another advanced idea at this time was Jefferson's plan for a solitary confinement prison in Virginia, antedating the work of the great criminal reformers in Europe. Jefferson describes his part in the design: "With respect to the plan of a Prison . . . I had heard of a benevolent society, in England, which had been indulged by the government, in an experiment of the effect of labor, in *solitary confinement*, on some of their criminals; which experiment had succeeded beyond expectation. The same idea had been suggested in France, and an Architect of Lyons (P.-G. Bugniet) had proposed a plan of a well-contrived edifice, on the principle of solitary confinement. I procured a copy, and as it was too large for our purposes, I drew one on a scale less extensive. . . . Its principle . . . but not its exact form, was adopted by Latrobe in carrying the plan into execution."

From his arrival in Europe in 1784 until he left in 1789 Jefferson used every opportunity for travel and to study the buildings and gardens of the Continent and England. He disliked French formal gardens but admired the natural style of the English, as well as the "Anglo-Chinese" gardens fashionable then in France. English architecture he thoroughly disapproved, but French buildings he loved, particularly the Hôtel de Salm, which he watched rise in 1785, and the Maison Carrée at Nîmes, at which he gazed "whole hours . . . like a lover at his mistress." From Lyons to Nîmes he was "nourished with the remains of Roman grandeur." In Germany he particularly admired buildings by French architects. But he never reached Rome or Vicenza, the home of Palladio, and never returned to the "eternal fogs" of Europe. The Hôtel de Salm was but one of the new, stylish, relatively small houses that the French nobility were building during the reign of Louis XVI. The members of the Court had tired of their great châteaux, and they wanted elegant, one-story pavilions, the emphasis being on comfort and privacy rather than magnificence.

Jefferson designed or planned changes in every house he ever lived in, and the beautiful Hôtel de Langeac on the Champs Élysées was no exception. Built by Jean F.-T. Chalgrin, this house was in the fashionable style of Louis XVI. It had oval rooms, comfortable bedrooms with their own dressing rooms, a sweeping stair, the importance of which was suppressed in an irregularly shaped room, and the latest style of plumbing, "Lieux à l'anglaise," or water closets. It was a luxurious and expensive house, yet not too large. Drawings by Jefferson show that he presumably designed its gardens in the informal "English" style of the period; and there is also a drawing of some of the interior rooms.

Jefferson was named Secretary of State after his return to America in 1789, and immediately attemped to set the impress of classical architecture on the new government buildings. As in the plan of Richmond, his ideas regarding the design of the streets and the Capitol, the President's House, the offices, and public walks were incorporated in a sketch plan, now in the Library of Congress. In this proposal he planned the whole community, and the design of its buildings was to be controlled by regulations and by land acquisition. In the drawing he indicated the sites of the President's House and the Capitol, both located now in much the same relationship to each other as he planned them. He proposed lot sizes fifty feet by the diagonal of the square but did not propose regularizing setbacks, believing they produced an ugly monotony. But he approved of uniform building heights, as they kept down the price of land, improved the houses, made the streets light and airy, and reduced the difficulty of fighting fires.

Jefferson not only helped L'Enfant, the designer of Washington, with ideas, but also lent him town plans he had collected abroad— Frankfurt, Karlsruhe, Amsterdam, Strasbourg, Paris, Orléans, Bordeaux, Lyons, Montpellier, Marseilles, Turin, and Milan. After Washington accepted the L'Enfant plan, Jefferson eagerly backed it.

Jefferson wrote to L'Enfant his preference for the adoption for the Capitol of some model of antiquity which had "the approbation of thousands of years." For the President's House he would prefer "the celebrated fronts of modern buildings, which have already received the approbation of all good judges. Such are the Galerie du Louvre, the Gardes meubles, and the two fronts of the Hôtel de Salm." He even tried to combine all of these in a design for it and anonymously submitted another, based on Palladio's Villa Rotonda, in the design competition.

As early as 1792, if not before he left France (for there is a drawing showing an enlarged house and a new garden which dates from 1785-1789), Jefferson had begun to think of remodeling and enlarging Monticello. The subtlety of French taste and its return to Roman Classicism under Louis XVI appealed to him strongly. As first constructed, Monticello must have seemed provincial and old-fashioned, and he determined to enlarge it, to add a mezzanine, skylights, and the "alcove bedrooms to which I am much attached," and to make it appear to be a one-story house (No. 14).

He described the effect he was after: "All the new and good houses are of a single story. That is of the height of 16. or 18 f. generally, and the whole of it given to rooms of entertainment; but in the parts where there are bedrooms they have two tiers of them of from 8. to 10. f. high each, with a small private staircase. By these means great staircases are avoided, which are expensive and occupy a space which would make a good room in every story." Here we have the answer to the question as to why Jefferson made his stairs so small and hidden: they were cheaper and took up less room.

The house as it stood in 1796 is shown in No. 3; the general design of the enlarged plan is shown in No. 15, in which the house is doubled in width. The eastern front of the old house had a transverse hall added along its length and rooms in front of that. The old portico was thus moved out beyond its original position. The suppression of the stairs indicated that this was meant to look like a one-story house, and they are placed in a logical position, although they are rather cramped because of the facilities Jefferson was trying to install. But the minimized stairs offer privacy, a luxury that was almost unknown in eighteenth-century America. That luxury is also evident in the elegant and comfortable accommodations for himself, which included a private toilet whose pot was removed via the air tunnel on a cart without ever being carried through the rooms. His bed was placed in an alcove open on both sides for ventilation.

The general plan is strikingly similar to that of the Hôtel Beaugeon in Paris, built in 1781, which he may have studied. Influenced by Louis

XVI and the Adams, the interior ornaments are based on the friezes shown in Desgodetz, *Édifices anciens de Rome*, and in his own copy of Errard and de Chambray's *Parallèle de l'Architecture antique et Moderne*, still in the Library of Congress, where the plates meant for each room are marked in his own hand. Monticello's dome, rare in American domestic architecture, is based on Plate 43, *Select Architecture*, and Jefferson referred to the room under it as the sky room.

While Jefferson has been credited with designing a great many houses, there is documentary evidence for only a few. These include drawings for Edgehill, a one-story house begun before 1798. For his friend George Divers at Farmington (Nos. 19 and 20), near Charlottesville, he designed beautiful octagonal rooms and a portico before 1802. He also made some drawings, once supposed to have been for Edgehill and Shadwell (his father's house that burned in 1770) that correspond to the plan of Edgemont as it was built. There is another drawing once supposed to have been a study for Shadwell, which has been identified as another Farmington, built for John Speed at Louisville, Kentucky.

When Jefferson became President he lost no opportunity to influence public architecture. He redesigned Pennsylvania Avenue, subdividing it by rows of trees, which separated the street from the sidewalks and from the proposed canal. He saw to it that Benjamin Henry Latrobe, trained in England, was appointed Surveyor of the Public Buildings. When work was pushed on the Capitol, both Jefferson and Latrobe wished to make some changes, which were later carried out, in the designs. No. 18 shows a tracing Jefferson made of Hallet's plan. No doubt he preferred the central court in this design to the impracticality of Thornton's central portion, and the copy was made so that Jefferson could study changes. There is also a design for the same building in which the French Panthéon was his inspiration. For the President's House he suggested to Latrobe a great semi-circular portico, and the bed alcove on the main floor was undoubtedly his idea. In 1802-1803 he employed George Hadfield, Maria Cosway's brother, to design on Judiciary Square a jail for solitary confinement. As President he set his stamp of approval on classical architecture for the nation's capital and selected the best-trained architects he could find to execute it.

Before, during, and after the Presidency Jefferson also found time for further revisions at Monticello and for various houses for his friends. But with his beloved Monticello he was constantly preoccupied. By 1792 he was about to resume the finishing "of my house" and was ordering materials. In 1794 he had complained to George Wythe that "We are now living in a brick kiln, for my house, in its present state, is nothing better." Short of cash, he started a nailery in 1795. In 1796 he wrote to Volney that "my house, which had never been more than half finished, had, during a war of eight years and my subsequent absence of ten years, gone into almost total decay. I am now engaged in repairing, altering and finishing it." Also in 1796 he was working on details of the "sky room" under the dome, which indicate his methods of designing in which the proportions of a room are fixed to the proportions of a particular order. While the first version of Monticello was based mainly on Palladio with some details from Gibbs, the interiors of the second version are based on Errard and de Chambray and on Desgodetz.

The next few years were years of frustration in spite of the fact that James Dinsmore, a skilled workman, was brought from Philadelphia in 1798. In 1801 James Oldham, another experienced workman, was employed, and a great deal was accomplished. In June, 1802, Jefferson explained the space over his bed, the subject of so much mythmaking: "the intention of the framing over my bed in the chamber was to enable us to have a room above the chamber if it should ever be desired." In 1804 Oldham was directed to construct, between the hall and the parlor, the unique folding glass doors that operate on a bicycle-type sprocket, one door moving when the other is opened. Also in 1804 another excellent workman, James Neilson, of Philadelphia, was employed.

By 1805, when work was well along on the final revision of the house, Jefferson had turned to Monticello's landscape; the farm was to be set into as formal a pattern as possible, withal retaining a practical consideration of rural life. (In 1765 he had acquired William Shenstone's works and by 1771 Whatley's *Observations* on modern gardening.) He was the first American to propose a garden in the landscape style. The top of the mountain was to be laid out with lawns and groves of trees arranged to frame the views from the roundabouts, or paths which circled the hill. The side of the mountain was to be turned into a *ferme ornée*, and there was to be a labyrinth of broom in a pinwheel design. Dells and glens were included to carry out the landscape ideas of Shenstone in England, whose estate, The Leasowes, Jefferson had visited in 1786. Because of Jefferson's straitened circumstances, Fiske Kimball reasoned that few of these improvements, beyond the round-

abouts and the separation of the entrance roads from the great terraced lawn to the southwest of the house, were ever carried out. However, Jefferson did order bricks for a garden temple (Nos. 5 and 6). We do not know which it was, as he had planned "a specimen of Gothic, a model of the Pantheon, model of cubic architecture, a specimen of Chinese." The Maison Carrée was chosen for cubic architecture, and the Monument of Lysicrates, based on the drawings of Stuart and Leroy.

Jefferson's little granddaughter, Ellen Randolph, wrote him in 1808 that "the hall with the gravel-coloured border is the most beautiful room I ever was in, without excepting the Drawing rooms at Washington." As it also housed his Indian relics and mammoth bones, Jefferson on one occasion called it "a kind of Indian Hall." While the house was essentially finished in 1809, the railings on the terraces were not completed until 1824, and as late as 1825 six cases of chimney "pilas" arrived for it.

Years before, in 1803, Jefferson had taken Robert Mills to Monticello as an architectural student. No. 14 is Mills's drawing of the finished house. At the University of Virginia are some studies by Mills of designs by Jefferson for a *villa rotonda*, probably exercises. The porticoes have only four columns each, with octagonal bays on the sides, making this the freest version and most practical of Jefferson's essays in the rotunda form (No. 16). The University also has some studies made about 1780 for the Governor's House in Richmond. Here there are shown the main story and the second floor, and two four-column porticoes. This plan is more traditional, for there are two wings, one containing the kitchen and the other a laundry connected to the main block by short colonnades.

Thus Jefferson experimented with the rotunda form in four versions for residential purposes: about 1772-1781 for the Governor's House in Williamsburg, about 1780 for the Governor's House in Richmond, in 1792 in the competition for the President's House in Washington, and again in 1803. None of these was to be realized, not even the dome on Barboursville (No. 22), which he designed in 1817. Only at Monticello was he able to construct a domed house.

In 1806 Jefferson settled on an octagonal plan (Nos. 29 and 30), the first in America for residential purposes, for his retreat at Poplar Forest, and by 1809 he was able to stay in the house, although it was not painted until 1817, and the final ornaments for it were not ordered until 1822. At any rate, the scheme of Poplar Forest is very successful, with its large, square dining room surrounded by octagonal rooms with bed alcoves. The highly centralized pyramidal form is very handsome. The grounds were carefully laid out to repeat the form of the octagon: there was a forecourt of clipped yew, and on the south a sunken lawn bordered by terraces planted with trees. This is a most skillful and sophisticated design, whose parts are carefully related. Bremo has sometimes been credited to Jefferson. It seems he did make suggestions, but John Neilson is cited as the architect in the cornerstone. He along with James Dinsmore came from Philadelphia to work at Monticello (Nos. 31, 32). He designed Ampthill for Randolph Harrison in Cumberland County in 1815. Two years later Barboursville (No. 22) was designed for James Barbour in Orange County.

The great achievement of Jefferson's architectural career was the University of Virginia (No. 26). As early as 1804-1805 he had been considering buildings in the form "of an academical village rather than of one large building." By 1810 his ideas had crystallized into a complex of buildings with "a small and separate lodge for each professorship, with only a hall below for his class, and two chambers above for himself; joining these lodges by barracks for a certain portion of the students, opening into a covered way to give a dry communication between all the schools. The whole of these arranged around an open square of grass or trees." Probably the general scheme was inspired by viewing Louis XVI's favorite château at Marly, which he had visited with Maria Cosway when in Paris. There the Sun King's pavilion was an axis, and six separate pavilions formed a row on either side of a broad expanse of grass, one for each of the twelve months.

Jefferson had written to Dr. William Thornton, asking for his opinions. Thornton suggested, among other things, columns instead of piers for the colonnades, pavilions at the corners of the quadrangle to express the change of direction, and porticoes over arcades.

Jefferson then wrote to B. H. Latrobe, whose most important idea was a focal building, preferably a rotunda, which Jefferson adopted eagerly. While Jefferson wrote from Monticello on October 14, 1817, to Latrobe that he would select the fronts of the next two pavilions from his designs, he also wrote on his drawings for VIII and IX the word "Latrobe," and certainly his influence seems more apparent in these two pavilions than in the former two. Jefferson also found that his site would not allow the square he had originally planned, and so the Lawn itself was made into a long rectangle.

Jefferson not only designed the buildings and supervised their construction, with all the attendant difficulties of securing proper materials and competent workmen: he also had to coax money from a reluctant government and keep frugal legislators from changing his designs. They were continually pressing for a single large building, but as Jefferson wrote to Thornton, "instead of building a magnificent house which would exhaust all our funds, we propose to lay off a square . . . the outside of which we shall arrange [with] separate pavilions." Clearly he set forth his high goals: "the great object of our aim from the beginning has been to make the establishment the most eminent in the United States. . . . We have proposed therefore to call to it characters of the first order of science from Europe . . . but by the distinguished scale of its structure and preparation . . . to induce them to commit their reputations to it. . . . To stop where we are is to abandon our high hopes, and become suitors to Yale and Harvard for their secondary characters."

On October 7, 1822, five years after the cornerstone was laid, Jefferson was able to report not only his plans but the manner in which the University would function: "[We] have completed all the buildings proposed . . . ten distinct houses or pavilions containing each a lecturing room, with generally four other apartments and the accommodation of a professor and his family, and with a garden, and the requisite family offices; six hotels for dieting the students, with a single room in each for a refectory, and two rooms, a garden and offices for the tenant, and an hundred and nine dormitories, sufficient each for the accommodation of two students, arranged in four distinct rows between the pavilions and hotels, and united with them by covered ways; which buildings are all in readiness for occupation, except that there is still some plaistering to be done now in hand, which will be finished early in the present season, the garden grounds and garden walls [No. 28] to be completed, and some columns awaiting their capitals not yet received from Italy. . . . The remaining building . . . which was to contain rooms for religious worship, for public examinations, for a library and other associated purposes. . . . [The Rotunda] is not begun for want of funds." It was begun in 1823 and was far enough along for the University to open its doors for the first time in 1825.

While the exterior design of the Rotunda was based upon that of the Pantheon in Rome, simplified and reduced to one-half the scale of the original, the interior was divided into two floors with a high basement.

The dome room for the library was conceived as a section of a sphere, suggesting the proportions of the original. No. 27 admirably illustrates Jefferson's success in enclosing a monumental and functional interior in a predetermined form.

With its three great oval rooms on the main floor and its free form hall, the Rotunda had the finest suite of oval rooms in America (No. 26). Possibly the idea for the design of ovals in a circle came from the Désert de Retz, which Jefferson had visited with Maria Cosway. After the fire of 1895 and over the protests of the faculty, the interior was completely changed when the building was rebuilt by Stanford White. Plans are now being made to restore this focal structure of Jefferson's magnificent complex of buildings to its former grandeur. For the domed ceiling of the circular library he planned a planetarium. He would paint the dome sky blue and set gilt stars and planets against it; there would be a seat for an operator, and the stars could be changed to conform to their varying positions. His specification book also gives insights into his care as a designer. With the Rotunda dominating the northern end, the Lawn opened to a vista of the mountains. It was closed when Stanford White built Cabell Hall and its flanking laboratories in 1898-1902.

The pavilions (Nos. 23, 24, and 25) themselves he wished to make "models of taste and good architecture, and of a variety of appearance, no two alike, so as to serve as specimens for the Architectural lecturer," as he wrote to Dr. Thornton. Their orders were based on Errard and de Chambray's *Parallèle de l'Architecture* and Palladio. To increase the apparent length of the Lawn, he enlarged the distance between each one as they are located farther from the Rotunda. In the French manner he terminated his great Lawn with small porticoes *à point*, which frame the terminal pavilions.

On October 6, 1817, in the presence of Jefferson, Madison, and Monroe the cornerstone of Pavilion VII, West Lawn, was laid. This design is amazingly similar to his early designs for Monticello. He made several studies for it, and one is shown in No. 23. Jefferson experimented unsuccessfully with local stone and even imported workmen. The capitals these men produced were not satisfactory, and he had to import others.

In 1819 Jefferson wrote that he was beginning drawings for the pavilions on East Lawn. Pavilion II (No. 24), whose order was taken from the "Ionic of Fortuna Virilis," has a plan from *Select Architecture*,

an example of Jefferson's method of putting two dissimilar elements together. In this masterly plan, a small entry is provided to shield the rooms from draughts. The large schoolroom is beautifully proportioned with alcoves on either end of the fireplace. When this pavilion was restored in recent years, it was found that the stair and the rooms were framed exactly as shown on Jefferson's drawing. However, this was not always true, and it is of great interest in studying these drawings to discover how much of his projected designs he was actually able to build.

For covering the dormitories Jefferson planned to use flat roofs, despite protests of some members of the Board of Visitors, over which he presided as Rector. He called them rooflets and built them of valleys of wood about eighteen inches deep covered with tin, like a series of gutters. He had already used this form of construction to cover the wings of Monticello. In time the "rooflets" leaked, and pitched roofs of slate were substituted. About 1840 the original wood railings rotted out and were replaced by the present cast iron ones, in which is set a pattern of Gothic arches. On the second floors of all the pavilions, Franklin stoves were installed. Having experimented with Rumford fireplaces at Monticello, Jefferson believed stoves would be even more efficient. The two parallel rows of ranges had three pavilions each, for student dining halls. In at least one building Jefferson wanted "some French family of good character, wherein it is proposed that the boarders shall be permitted to speak French only, with a view to their becoming familiarised to conversation in that language." The students' rooms between the dining halls, or hotels, as Jefferson called them, open on arcades, not colonnades, and their proportions are taken almost directly from Palladio.

In 1818 and 1821, in the midst of his plans for the University, Jefferson made drawings for courthouses in Botetourt and Buckingham Counties. He also designed the original Christ Church in Charlottesville, which was finished in 1826, the year he died. The design is clearly based upon that of St. Philippe du Roule by Chalgrin in Paris, which was near his Paris house.

Because of the grandeur of Jefferson's career as statesman, his architecture has been overshadowed. Yet had he done nothing else, he would be remembered today for his distinguished buildings, as the representative drawings here reproduced and the descriptive notes at the end of this booklet so amply illustrate.

While the Roman Revival was largely his contribution, he stimulated the Greek Revival, a product of the "Greek fever" engendered by the Greek War for Independence. Prosperous planters from the South passed through Charlottesville on their way to summer at the Virginia springs. Undoubtedly the white columns of the temple houses at the University had a strong influence on those classical houses that sprang up all over the old South. Jefferson established so strongly the classical tradition for public buildings that it persists even today, unfortunately often in watered-down versions. Whenever he could he pushed the arts and befriended artists. He encouraged the education of artists and architects. He was the leading Romantic Classicist in America before Latrobe, and such was his devotion to antiquity that he even promoted the temple form before it became popular in Europe. At the same time he was constructing the Rotunda at the University, buildings based on the Pantheon were rising all over Europe, thus putting him in the forefront of the classical surge of the decade from 1815 to 1825. To America, where the English vernacular of Sir Christopher Wren had been the tradition, he brought the Roman Revival, as interpreted by the French classicists and by Palladio. But the native American materials and traditions of craftsmanship helped transform his buildings into something new: Roman and French classicism interpreted in red brick, white painted wood, and stucco.

Like all important artists, Jefferson was capable of growth. While the first version of Monticello was exceptional, unique in the colonies for its adherence to Palladianism, it was still a provincial seat. After the impact of Europe and the influence of his architectural library, the finished Monticello was a highly civilized and sophisticated design: a remarkable record of one man's experiment in the art of living. If he were alive today he would no doubt take great interest in modern architecture.

While no other American house, and few in Europe, so well express the character of its builder and architect, the design of Monticello represents the mathematical mind of a leading exponent of the age of reason whose scientific analysis of classical art produced carefully designed elements that do not always merge into a unified whole. On the other hand, he rises above this limitation in his town plans, at Poplar Forest, and at the University of Virginia. Even among European universities there is nothing to rival the last. The clarity and variety of the parts which relate so well to the entire composition, the brilliance of red brick and white trim, the serenity of the long colonnades climaxed by the majesty of the Rotunda—this is indeed a noble achievement. Jefferson stands alone, as the most distinguished native architect of the Early Republic.

FREDERICK DOVETON NICHOLS

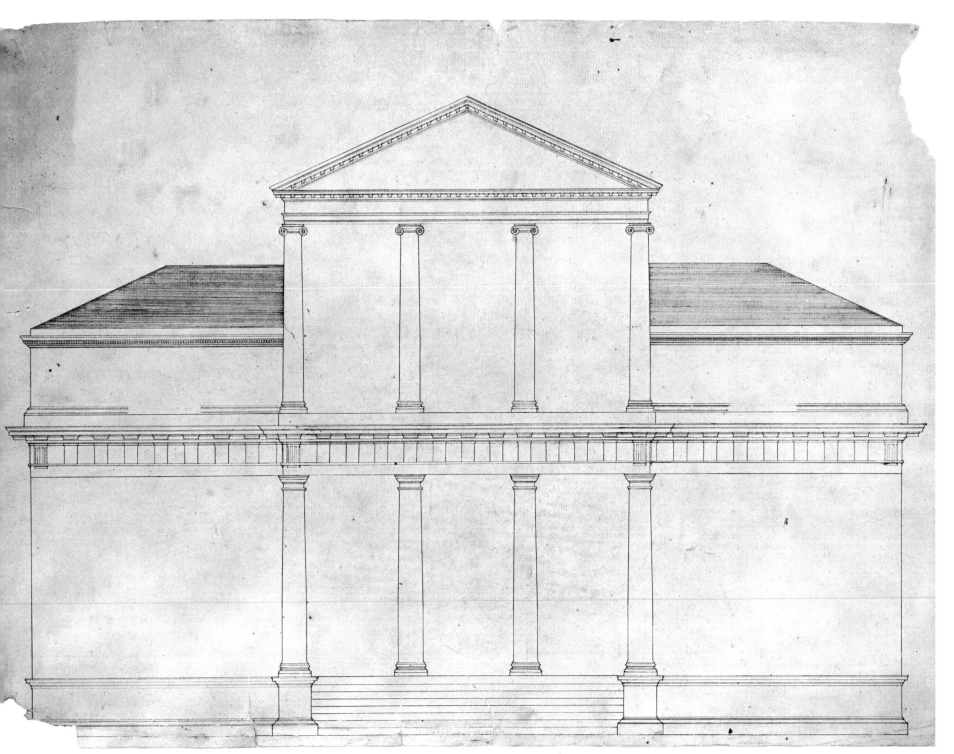

Monticello. Elevation, First Version (see 47)

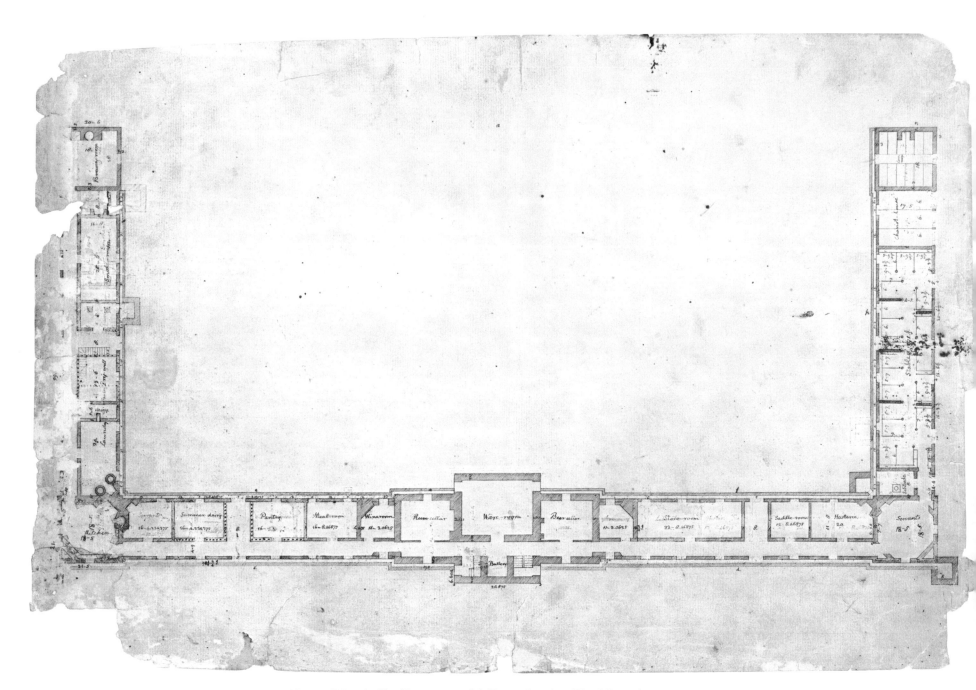

No. 2. Monticello: Basement with Dependencies, Final Drawing (see 56)

No. 3. Monticello: First Floor with Dependencies, Final Drawing (see 57)

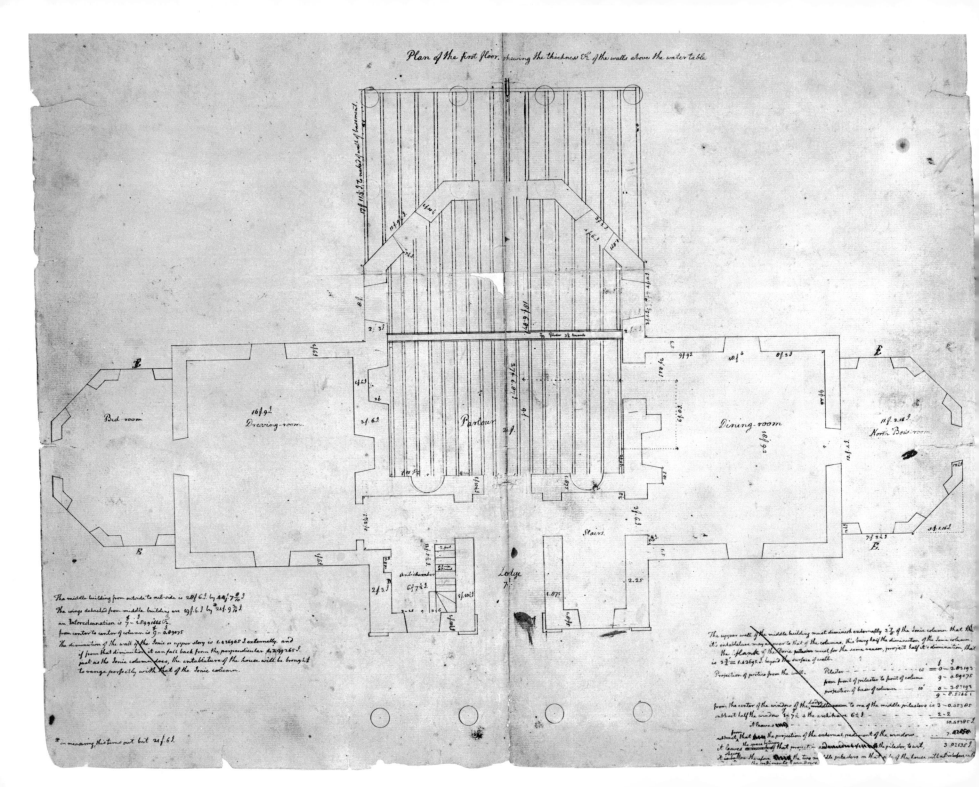

Plan of the first floor, shewing the thickness &c. of the walls above the water table

Bed room

Drawing-room

Parlour

Dining-room

North Bow-room

Antichamber

Stairs.

Lodge

No. 5. Monticello: Decorative Outchamber, Elevation (see 91)

The form & proportions of this building are taken from Jones's designs pl. 73. only that this is square

the figure of the key-stone is taken from Palladio B. 4. pl. 49

the manner of shingling from the Lanthern of Demosthenes 2. Spon's voiages pa. 132.

the fireplace of the room below must be at the N.E. end

the walls at the N.E. & S.W. ends must be 24.I. thick as high as the spring of the arch to support the arch for the two flues, which being each

12.I. by 14.I. will require the section of the bow to be 21.I. in the direction of the radius, & 23.I. horizontal.

the cieling of the room to be coved. 4 ways.

the basement = basement of the principal house.

the order above the basement 15.5.f. the module of the order would be 21¼ I.

projection of basement 3/10 of a foot

radius of the dome 8.8.f.

center of the dome is in the under line of the Cima recta of the Cornice.

the periphery of the dome is 140° of the circle.

the 3. plinths of the dome are 2.5.f high 'curit   the lowest 1.1.f   it's diameter 20.f.
                                                  the middle .75.f   it's diameter 18.75
                                                  the highest .65   it's diameter 17.65

the horizontal width of the dome at it's bottom 16.5.f.
          it's perpondicular height 5.8.f

the center of the chimney bow is 10.75.f. above the basement

the external cornice. Tuscan. 15.4.I high. the projection 15.234.I.

the internal work Tuscan. the perpondicular part of the wall being 10.75.f. the module will be 1.f.

the capping of the Pedestal is taken from Gibbs, the rest of it from the Builder's dictionary verbo 'Tuscan'

the basement 2.f.   the column (which is also the space for the window) 7.f. the Entablature 1.f. 9.I.

The Portico. Ionic with a Dentil cornice.

    the Column & entablature 10-48' = 10.8.f.

    the module of the order then is 1.f.

    the width of the Portico is 11. modules. there being 3. intercolonnations of 2½ modules each.

The Keystone will be 2.f.6.I. high; it's diameter where smallest at the neck 10.I. this will allow the princi-
    -pal perforation to be 7½.I. diam. besides this there must be 6. smaller perforations 5.I. diam.
    issuing at the upper side of the belly of the key stone. these seven perforations will be equal
    to one of 15.I. diam. which would be equal to two square flues of 9.I. each.
        for different forms of key stones. see In. Jones v.2. p.19. Palld. america's house.

the present floor of the Outchamber must remain as a foundation to the other floor, & the
    more effectually to prevent sounds below disturbing the room above.

Apr. 23. 1779. build such a temple as that in Jones pl. 78 on the point of land between
the meadow & intended fish pond in the park: & let Outchamber be on the old plan.

No. 6. Monticello: Decorative Outchamber, Specifications (see 91)

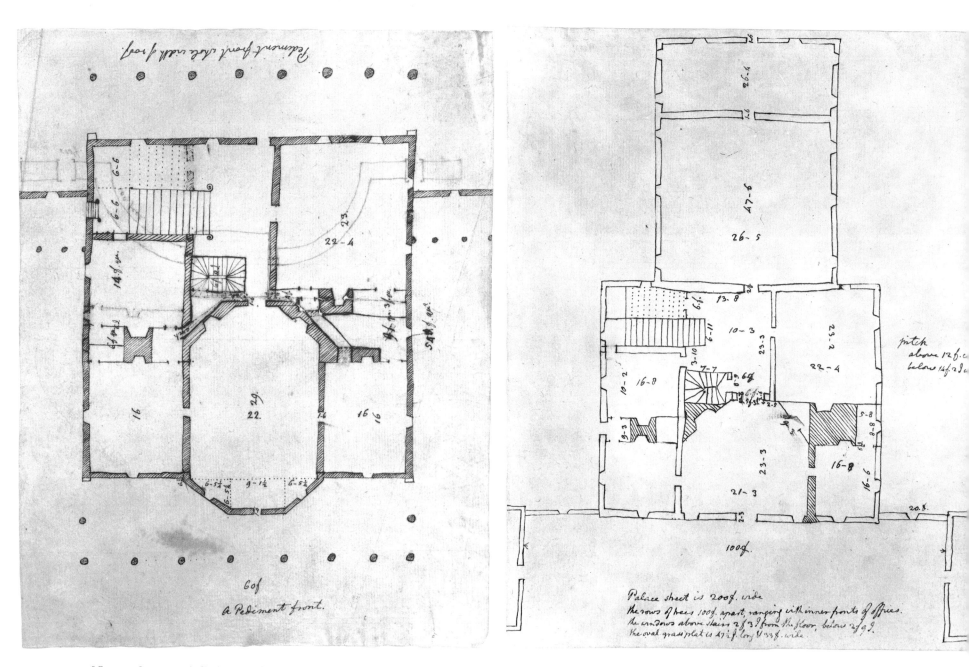

No. 7. Governor's Palace, Williamsburg: Plan (see 425)   No. 8. Governor's Palace, Williamsburg: Measured Drawing (see 422)

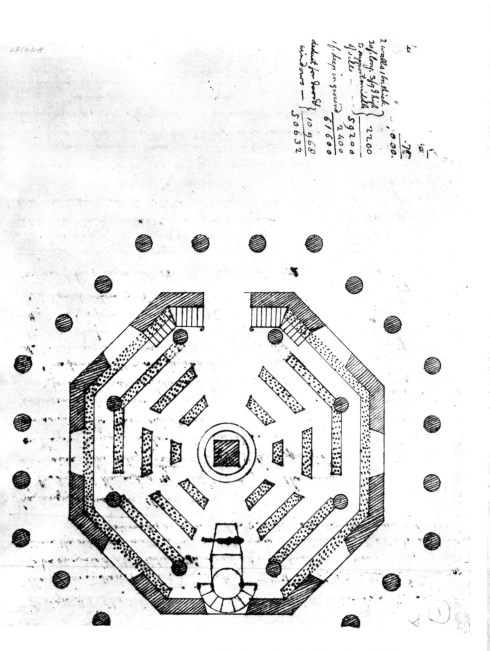

No. 9. Octagonal Chapel, Williamsburg?: Plan (see 419)

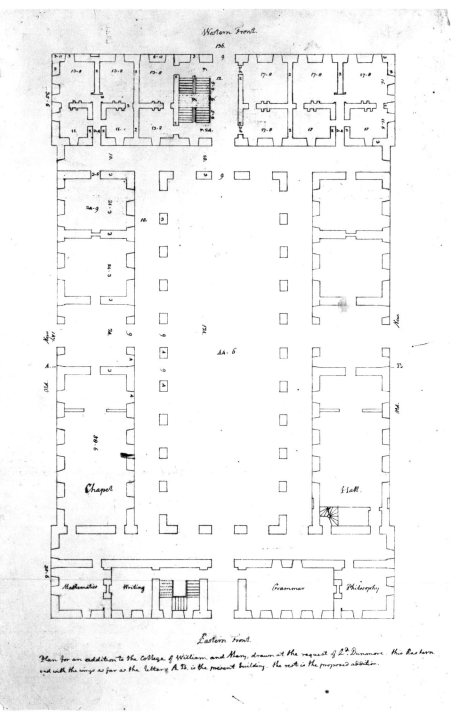

No. 10. College of William and Mary: Plan for Addition (see 421)

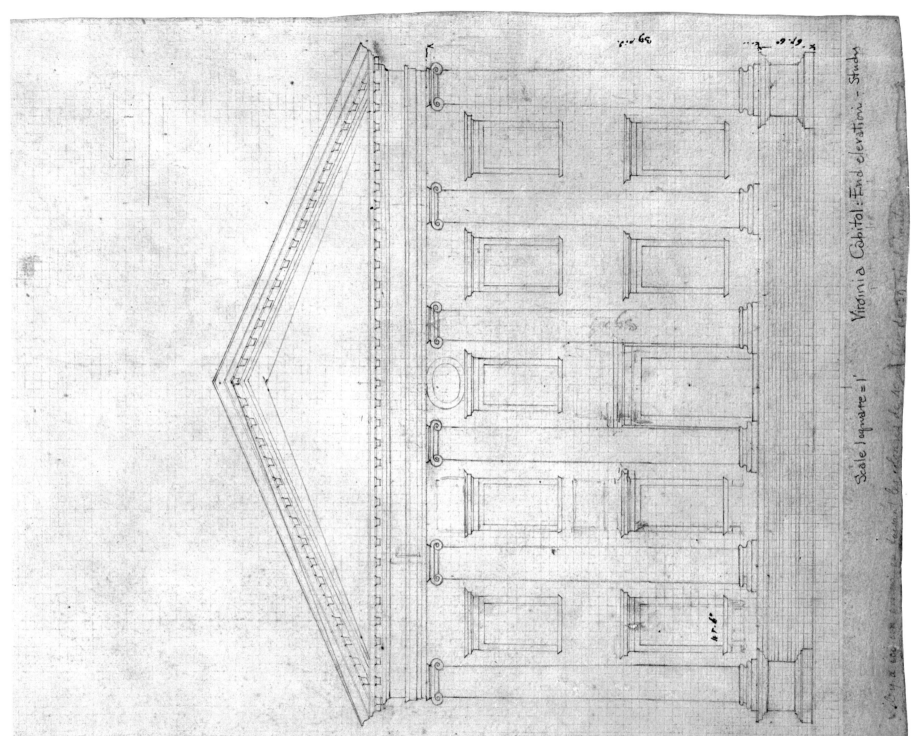

Scale 1 square = 1'   Virginia Capitol: End elevation - Study

No. 11. Virginia Capitol, Richmond: Front Elevation (see 279)

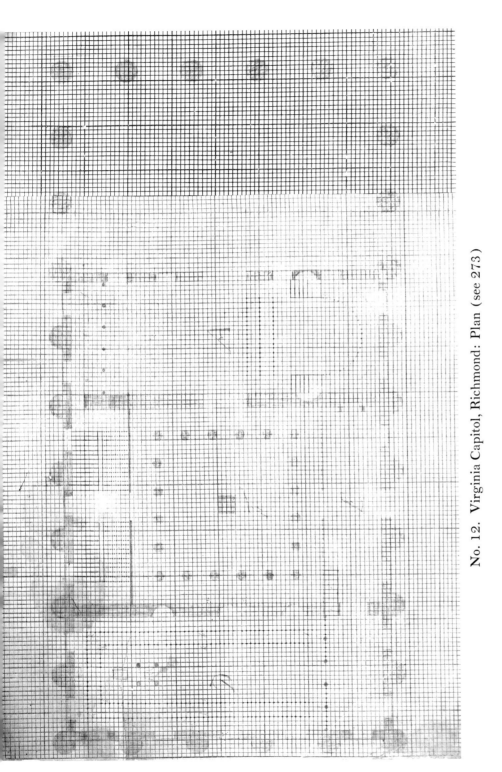

No. 12. Virginia Capitol, Richmond: Plan (see 273)

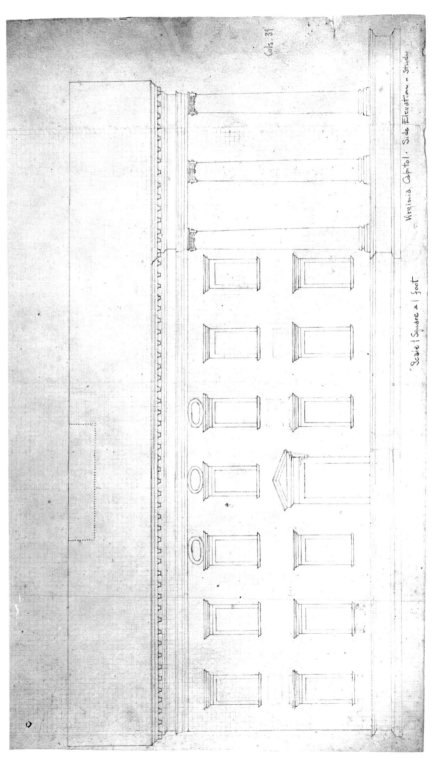

No. 13. Virginia Capitol, Richmond: Side Elevation (see 278)

No. 14. Monticello: West Elevation, Final Version (drawn by Robert Mills; see 154)

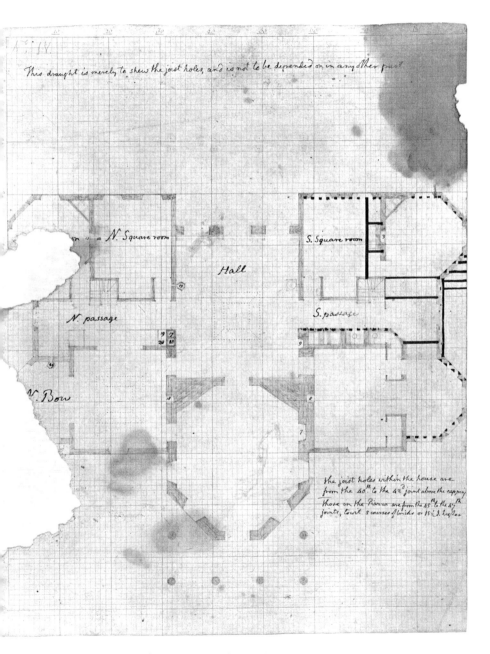

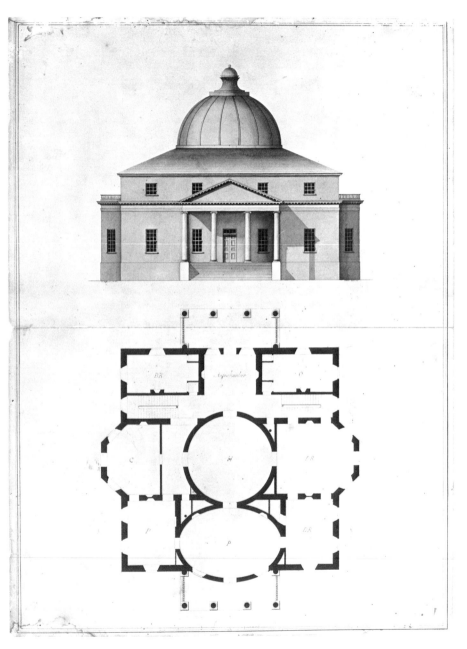

No. 15. Monticello: First Floor, Final Version (see 135)　　　　No. 16. A Rotunda House (drawn by Robert Mills; see 411)

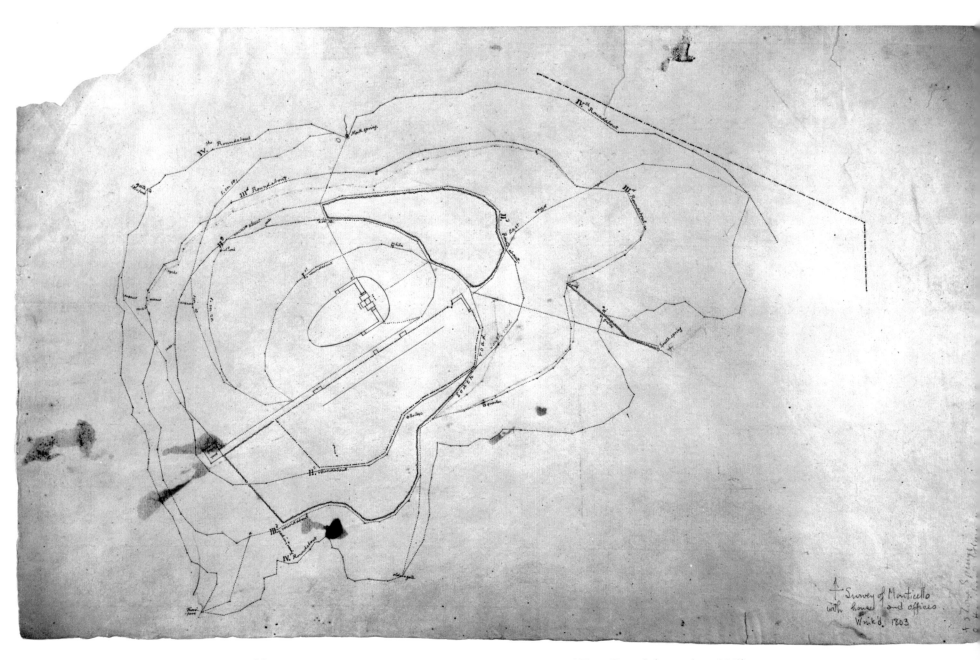

No. 17. Monticello: Survey showing House, Offices, and Four Roundabouts (see 225)

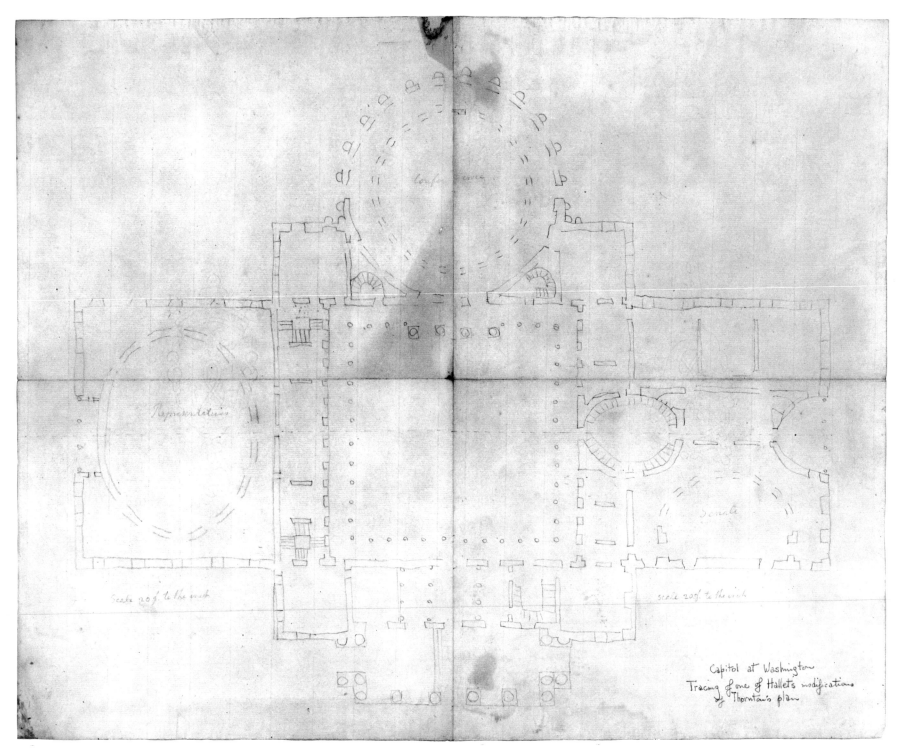

Representatives

Conference

Senate

Scale 20 f. to the inch

scale 20 f. to the inch

Capitol at Washington
Tracing of one of Hallet's modifications
of Thornton's plan

No. 12. Capitol, Washington; Jefferson's Tracing of Hallet's Plan (see 389)

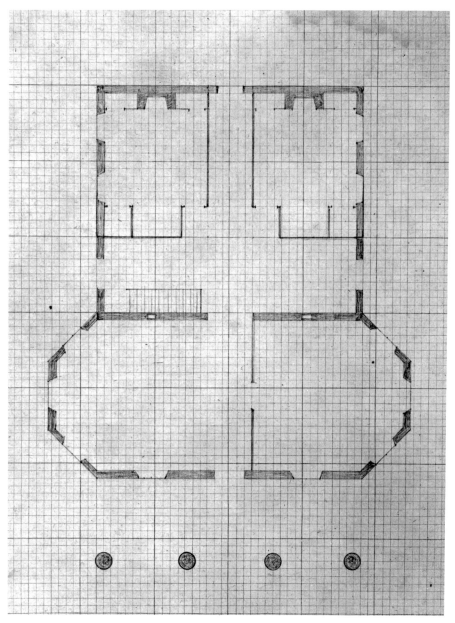

No. 19. Farmington, Charlottesville: Plan (see 14)

No. 20. Farmington, Charlottesville: Elevation (see 13)

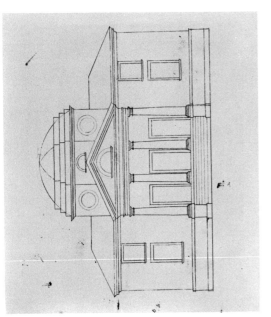

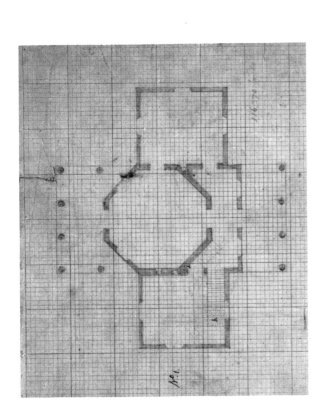

No. 21. Plan and Elevation for a Town House (see 4a)

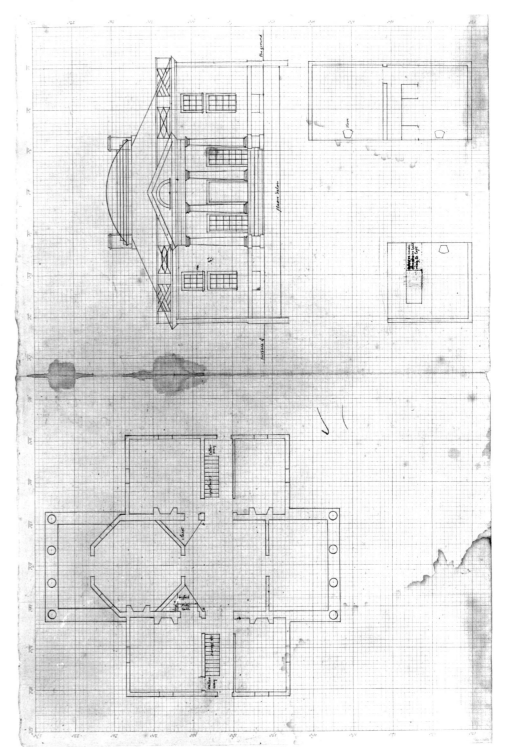

No. 22. Barboursville: Plan and Elevation (see 5)

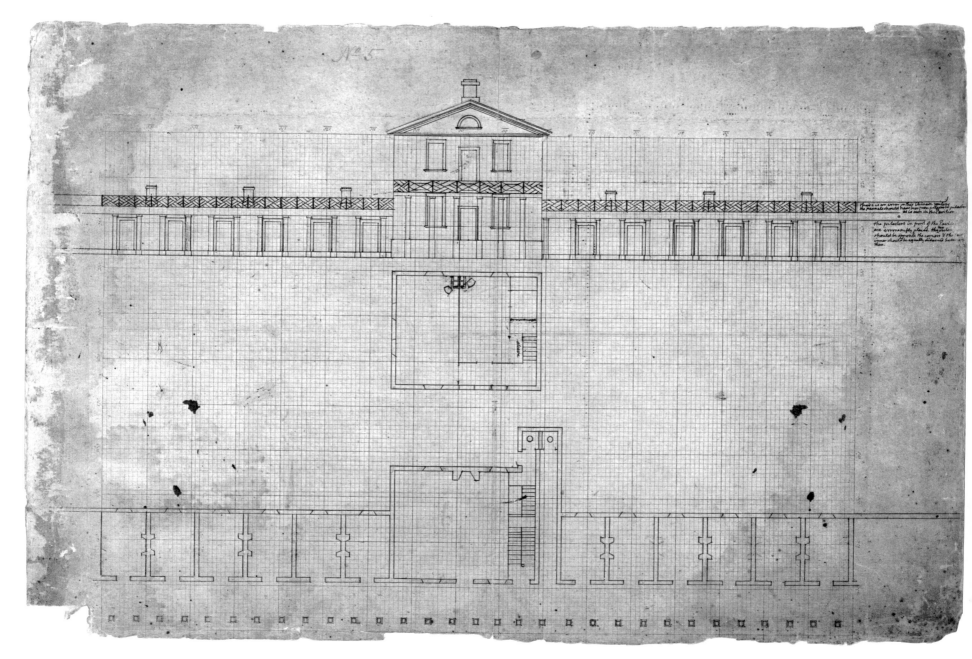

No. 23. University of Virginia: Pavilion VII (see 309)

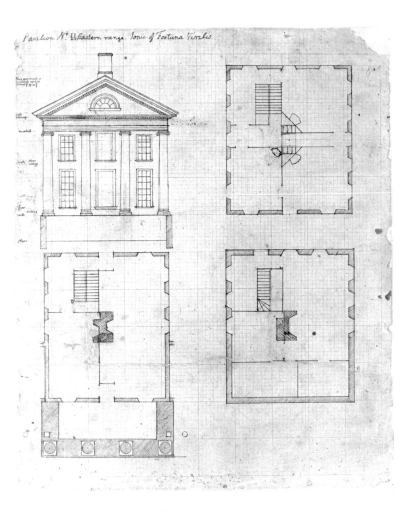

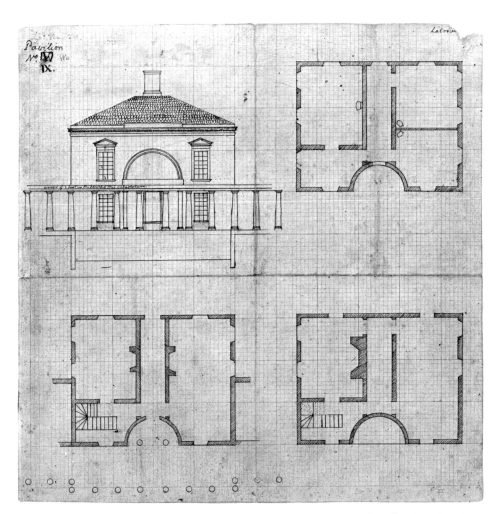

No. 24. University of Virginia: Pavilion II (see 321)   No. 25. University of Virginia: Pavilion IX (see 357)

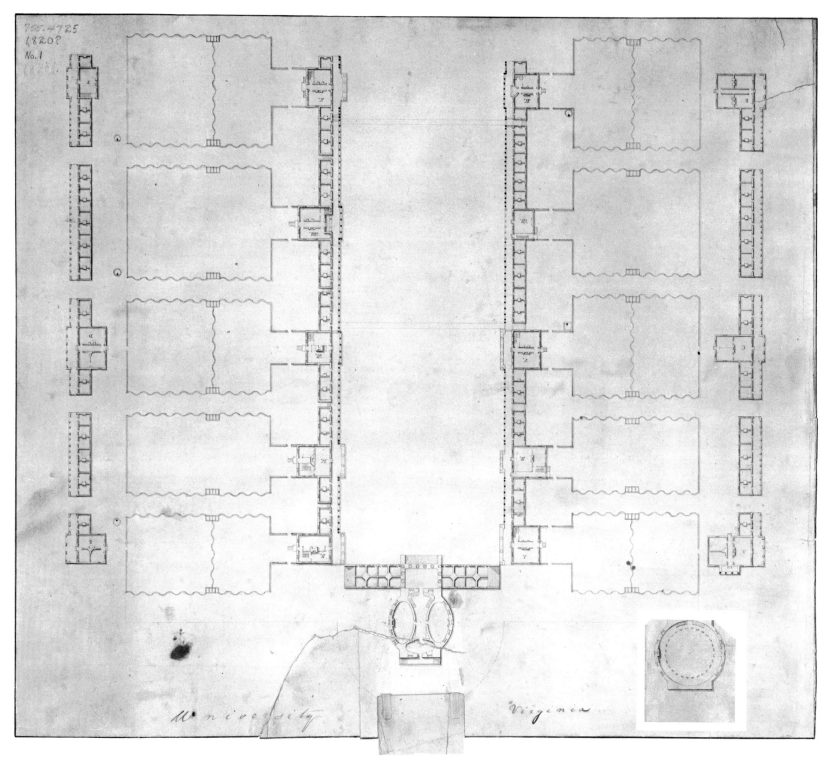

University   Virginia

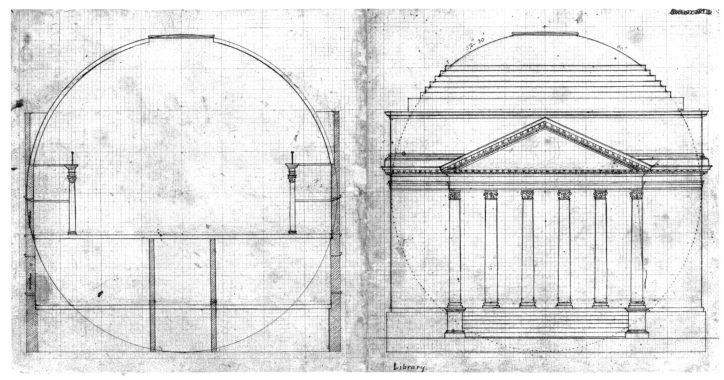

No. 27. University of Virginia: Rotunda, Section and Elevation (see 328 and 329)

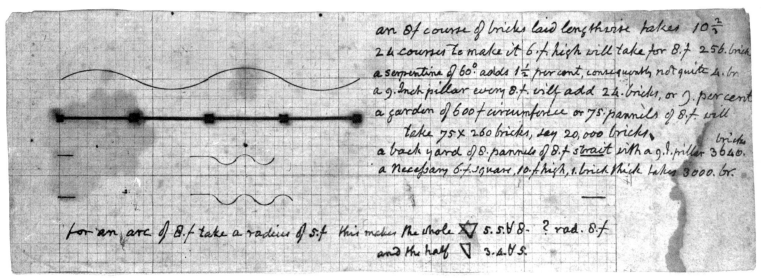

No. 28. University of Virginia: Serpentine Wall, Detail (see 315)

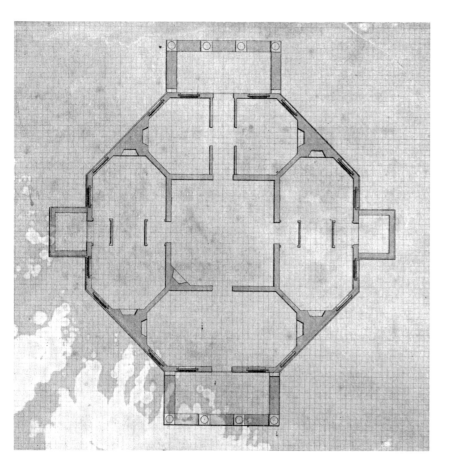

No. 29. Poplar Forest: Plan (see 350)

No. 30. Poplar Forest: Elevation (see 351)

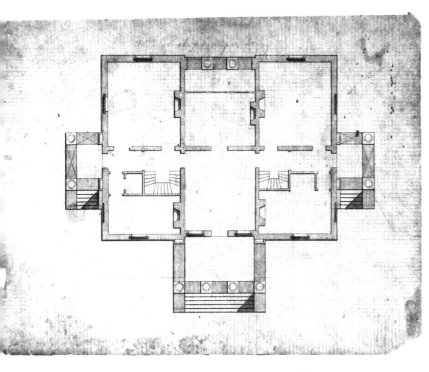

No. 31. Bremo: Plan (see 351a)

No. 32. Bremo: Elevation (see 351b)

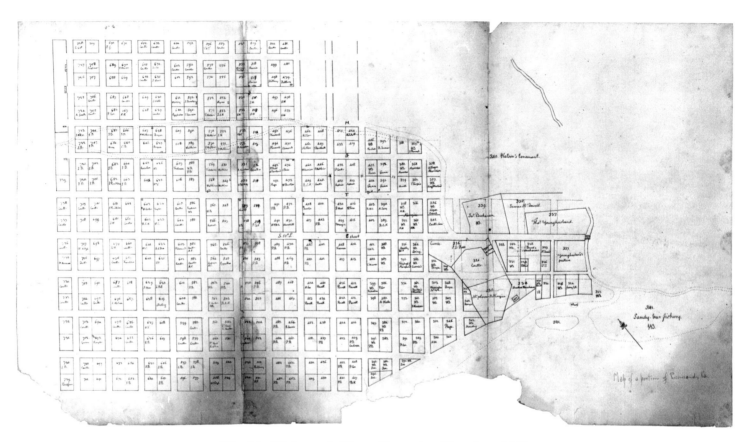

No. 33. Richmond: Town Extension Plan (see 293)

Check List of Thomas Jefferson's Architectural Drawings

THE check list that follows is arranged in alphabetical order by places or buildings. Important surveys only are listed after the same headings to which they belong. Structures without locations or names are placed alphabetically by types at the end. "K" before a number means the drawing is under that number in Fiske Kimball, *Thomas Jefferson, Architect* (Boston, 1916); "No." before a number refers to an illustration in this booklet; a number standing alone refers to an entry in this check list. The location abbreviations for the collections where drawings are deposited follow the usage of the National Union Catalog of the Library of Congress, as follows: CSmH, Henry E. Huntington Library; CtY, Yale University Library; DLC, Library of Congress; MdHi, Maryland Historical Society; MHi, Massachusetts Historical Society; MoHi, Missouri State Historical Society; Vi, Virginia State Library; ViMo, Monticello; ViU, University of Virginia Library; and ViWC, Colonial Williamsburg.

In his great folio, *Thomas Jefferson, Architect*, Fiske Kimball made a fundamental study of the drawing paper used by Jefferson, following the method recommended by Charles Moïse Briquet in his dictionary of watermarks, *Les Filigraines: Dictionnaire Historique des Marques du Papier dès leur Apparition vers 1282 jusqu'en 1600*, 4 vols. (Paris, 1907). The present study has been based upon Kimball's work, but the addition of numerous drawings he did not know has indicated in some cases a change in date and identification. Because of Jefferson's extensive correspondence supplies of paper lasted rarely longer than three years, although the co-ordinate papers, which were used only for drawings, lasted for a much longer period. Despite his use of "scraps" in 1809 after losing a trunk containing paper, a quantity of unused paper survived him when he died in 1826. In general, dated papers were used from four to six years after manufacture. Sizes of papers are given as average sizes rather than largest or smallest. (An index to papers Jefferson used follows the check list entries.)

Before Jefferson went to France in 1784, ink was the usual medium for his drawings. He probably adopted the hard, sharply pointed pencil after that date because Clérisseau and other professionals used it, although he still continued to use inks as well as co-ordinate papers. Ordinary writing ink was employed; it is now a medium shade of brown. India ink was occasionally used for washes.

Special acknowledgment should be made to Julian P. Boyd, L. H. Butterfield, and Walter Muir Whitehill for their encouragement and advice. The original idea for this booklet was theirs. Others who have given invaluable help are: James A. Bear, Jr., Francis L. Berkeley, Jr., Helen D. Bullock, Norma B. Cuthbert, Malcolm Freiberg, Dumas Malone, William B. O'Neal, Howard C. Rice, Jr., Stephen T. Riley, E. Millicent Sowerby, John C. Wyllie, and the staffs of the Alderman Library, the Library of Congress, and the Massachusetts Historical Society. For the conclusions which follow, the author accepts full responsibility.

F. D. N.

1. ANNAPOLIS. Hammond-Harwood house, measured drawings of the plan and elevation. Ink. Paper AZ. 9⅞ x 7⅞ in. 1783-1784. K107, MHi.

2. AMPTHILL. Ink and pencil. Scale: about 10' = 1". Paper BD. 8¾ x 10¼ in. 1815. K203, MHi.

3. ———. Ink. Paper CX. 4½ x 2½ in. 1815. K204, MHi.

4. UNIDENTIFIED TOWN HOUSE. Ink. Press copy from elevation in 4a. Paper CX. 8 x 10¾ in. K205, MHi.

4a. ———. Notes (2 pp.) and elevation in ink, plans of first and second floors and section in pencil. Ca. 1800, as the remodeling of Monticello is mentioned in the notes. These drawings, however, are not for Monticello, but for a house in town, probably Philadelphia. These drawings were evidently modified and submitted to James Barbour for Barboursville in 1817 as stated by Kimball in reference to the press copy above. ViU 10,264. (See No. 21.)

5. BARBOURSVILLE. This plan and elevation for James Barbour of Orange County, Virginia, show a house with a dome and portico. The dome was never built, and the house is now a ruin. Ink. Scale: about 10' = 1". Paper BD. Specifications on back. 20½ x 13⅛ in. 1817. K206, MHi. (See No. 22.)

6. EDGEHILL. Pencil. Scale: about 10' = 1". Paper BD. 8 x 11 in. Before 1798. K170, MHi.

7. EDGEMONT. Ink (press copy). Scale: about 10' = 1". Laid paper, illegible watermark. 8 x 11 in. About 1803-1806. This plan corresponds to Edgemont as built. K171, MHi.

8. ———. Pencil. Scale: about 10' = 1". Paper BD. 8 x 9½ in. About 1803-1806. K172, MHi.

9. ———. Plan. Ink. Scale: 5' = 1". Paper BU. 11¼ x 17¼ in. About 1803-1806. K173, MHi.

10. ———. Plan of basement. Ink. Scale: 5' = 1". Paper BY. 11¾ x 15¾ in. About 1803-1806. K174, MHi.

11. "Improvement of the house at Elkhill." Plans showing portico in antis. Ink and pencil. 4¼ x 4½ in. On back: Notes on Fluvanna parish. See also 52 and 53. Paper CX. CSmH9371.

12. Floor plans of houses: (1) Farmington? 5¼ x 4⅝ in.; (2) Study for Poplar Forest? Shows a room with screen columns. Paper BR. No scale. 5 x 6⅜ in.

1803? (3) Two small buildings, apparently a town house and stable. Laid paper watermarked RUN. No scale. 3 x 8⅛ in.; (4) A study for quarters in Philadelphia, similar to Solitude, Fairmount Park. Drawn on back of an engraved invitation. Paper AS. 4¾ x 7⅞ in. About 1776. CSmH9384.

13. FARMINGTON. This elevation, surmounted by a Chinese lattice railing, shows a Tuscan portico. Ink (press copy). Scale: about 10' = 1". Paper CL. 7¼ x 10¼ in. 1802 or earlier. K182, MHi. (See No. 20.)

14. ———. Plan of a house for George Divers, based on Jefferson's favorite octagonal forms. Scale: about 10' = 1". Paper BD. 8 x 11 in. 1802 or earlier. K183, MHi. (See No. 19.)

15. ———. Studies. Pencil. Scale: about 10' = 1". Laid paper not BD. 7 x 10 in. 1802 or earlier. K184, MHi.

16. GERMANY. Miscellaneous sketches for joists, window sash, towers, etc., in a manuscript entitled "Memoranda on a tour from Paris to Amsterdam." Paper CA. 8 5/16 x 9¾ in. March 3, 1788-April 15, 1788. ViWC.

17. HIGGENBOTHAM HOUSE. Albemarle County. Plan and notes for Miss Mary Higgenbotham. Same plan as Edgemont. Ink. Paper BD. 8½ x 10 in. About 1809? CSmH Brock 263.

18. HOLLAND. "Hope's House near Harlaem." Ink. Rough sketch in a manuscript entitled "Memoranda on a Tour from Paris to Amsterdam." Paper CA. 8 5/16 x 9¾ in. March 16, 1788. ViWC.

19-20. LOUISVILLE. Farmington. (Opposite sides of the same sheet.) Studies. Ink. Paper CX. 8 x 5 in. (See Fiske Kimball, "Jefferson's Designs for Two Kentucky Houses," Society of Architectural Historians, Journal, IX [1950], 14-16. Kimball first thought these were of Poplar Forest.) Probably before 1810. K189-K190, MHi.

21. ———. Farmington. Pencil. Scale: about 10' = 1". Paper BD. 9½ x 10 in. (See ibid., pp. 14-16.) K191, MHi.

22. ———. Farmington. Pencil. Scale: about 10' = 1". Paper BD. 8¾ x 11 in. About 1804. (See ibid., pp. 14-16.) K192, MHi.

23-24. MAYSVILLE. Court House, Buckingham County. (Opposite sides of the same sheet.) Ink. Scale: about 10' = 1". Paper BD. 8½ x 11½ in. 1821. K214-K215, MHi.

25. MONTICELLO. Earliest plan. Ink. Paper AC. 3¾ x 6 in. Probably 1767, certainly before February, 1770. (As Fiske Kimball calls this the earliest study in his Thomas Jefferson, Architect, p. 118, which it undoubtedly is, its date has been changed.) See 27. K4, MHi.

26. ———. Early study. Ink and pencil. Scale: 24' = 1". Paper CX. 4¼ x 6¼ in. Before 1770. Fiske Kimball told the author this was Monticello, not Brandon. Traced from Robert Morris, Select Architecture (London, 1757), Plate 3. K119, MHi.

27. ———. Early plan. Ink. Scale: 10' = 1". Paper AD. 12¼ x 7½ in. 1768-1770. (See Fiske Kimball, "Jefferson and the Public Buildings of Virginia. I. Williamsburg, 1770-1776," Huntington Library Quarterly, XII [1949], 116.) K5, MHi.

28. ———. Early plan. Ink. Scale: 10' = 1". Paper AE. 7¼ x 9 in. 1768-1770. (See ibid., p. 116.) K6, MHi.

29. ———. Early plan. Ink. Dimensions of the order. Paper AF. 1768-1770. (See ibid., p. 116.) K7, MHi.

30. ———. Studies of dependency plans. Ink. Scale: 10' = 1". Paper AC. 12 x 7¼ in. 1768-1770. (See ibid., p. 116.) K8, MHi.

31. ———. Studies of dependency plans. Ink. Scale: 20' = 1". Paper AE. 7¼ x 7 in. 1768-1770. (See ibid., p. 116.) K9, MHi.

32. ———. Studies of dependency plans. Ink. Scale: 10' = 1". Paper AG. 17¾ x 14½ in. 1768-1770. (See ibid., p. 116.) K10, MHi.

33. ———. Study of the plan. Ink. Scale: 5' = 1". Paper AB. 14½ x 11¾ in. 1768-1770. (See ibid., p. 116.) K11, MHi.

34. ———. Study of general layout. Ink. Scale: 80' = 1". Paper AG. 9 x 14½ in. 1768-1770. (See ibid., p. 116.) K12, MHi.

35. ———. Study of a pavilion. Ink. Paper AG. 3½ x 3½ in. 1768-1770. (See ibid., p. 116.) K13, MHi.

36. ———. Study of a pavilion. Ink. Scale: 4′ = 1″. Paper not CX but AO. 13¾ x 11 in. 1768-1770. (See *ibid.*, p. 116.) K14, MHi.

37. ———. Plan of existing dining room in main house, not plan of first pavilion. Ink. Scale: 4′ = 1″. Paper AH. 12¼ x 7½ in. 1768-1770. (See *ibid.*, p. 116.) K15, MHi.

38. ———. Stone (or weaver's or overseer's) house. Ink. Paper AD. 7½ x 6¾ in. September, 1770. K16, MHi.

39. ———. Study for stone (or weaver's or overseer's) house. Ink. Paper AI. 3¾ x 6¼ in. September, 1770. K17, MHi.

40. ———. Study for the plan. Ink. Scale: 4′ = 1″. Paper AJ. 19 x 13¼ in. 1768-1770. (See *ibid.*, p. 116.) K18, MHi.

41. ———. Study for the elevation. Ink. Scale: 4′ = 1″. Paper AK. 26½ x 18¾ in. 1768-1770. (See *ibid.*, p. 116.) K19, MHi.

42. ———. Study for exterior doors on the west of the house (parlor and study). Ink. Scale: 4′ = 1″. Paper AL. 19 x 11¾ in. About 1770. K20, MHi.

43. ———. Plan of the cellars to accompany 40. (On back of 42.) Ink. Scale: 4′ = 1″. 23¾ x 18¾ in. Probably from 1770. K21, MHi.

44. ———. "Plan of the cellar floors." Ink. Scale: 4′ = 1″. Paper AL and AB. 23¾ x 14¼ in. Probably early in 1771. K22, MHi.

45. ———. Plan after James Gibbs, *Book of Architecture* (London, 1728), Plate 68. Ink. Paper CX. 2½ x 8 in. 1767-1769. CSmH9364.

46. ———. Sketch of elevation for first version. Plan on reverse. Paper CX. 4½ x 5½ in. 1769-1770. ViMo.

47. ———. Study for final elevation of the first version. Ink. Scale: 4′ = 1″. Paper AK. 18¾ x 13½ in. 1771-1772. ViU. (See No. 1.)

48. ———. Final elevation of first version. Scale: 4′ = 1″. Paper AL. 20 x 13½ in. Probably before March, 1771. K23, MHi. (See Cover.) The house

was nearly finished by 1782, but the upper portico seems never to have been completed. The octagonal ends are not shown on this drawing.

49. ———. Final first-floor plan of the first version of the house based on 40 and derived from Robert Morris' *Select Architecture*. The octagonal bows were added to this plan, showing the house as it was built. Ink. Scale: 4′ = 1″. Paper AL. 23¾ x 19½ in. Probably before March, 1771. K24, MHi. (See No. 4.)

50. ———. Working drawings for main stairs as shown on 57. Ink. Scale: 2′ = 1″. Paper AC. 7¼ x 10⅞ in. Probably 1771. K25, MHi.

51. ———. Working drawings for main stairs as shown on 57. Ink. Scale: 2′ = 1″. Paper AC. 7¼ x 10⅞ in. Probably 1771. K26, MHi.

52. ———. Study for the house showing wings with bays connected by quadrants, suggested by 119. Ink. Paper AH. 7½ x 3¼ in. Probably 1770 and early 1771. See also 11. K27, MHi.

53. ——— (on back of 52). Study for the house with wings, with bays connected by quadrants, suggested by 119. Ink. Probably 1770 and early 1771. K28, MHi.

54. ———. Studies for the house. Ink. Paper CX. 4⅛ x 4½ in. Probably 1770 and early 1771. K29, MHi.

55. ———. First study for dependencies. Ink. Paper AD. 7¼ x 5¾ in. 1771 or 1772. K30, MHi.

56. ———. Final drawing of the basement and dependencies. Ink. Scale 15′ = 1″. 20¾ x 13⅜ in. Before August 4, 1772. K31, MHi. (See No. 2.)

57. ———. Final drawing of the first floor with dependencies, showing octagonal buildings at the corners, and pavilions at the end of the U-shaped composition. Octagonal bows are part of original drawing. Ink. Scale: 15′ = 1″. Paper AM. 20¾ x 13½ in. Before August 4, 1772. K32, MHi. (See No. 3.)

58. ———. Plan of kitchen. Ink. Scale: 6′ = 1″. Paper AP. 7⅝ x 12½ in. 1771 or earlier. CSmH-9363.

59. ———. Studies for plans for dependencies with

brick estimates. Ink. 4⅝ x 3½ in. August 2, 1771. CSmH9365.

60. ———. "A section across the offices" (dependencies). Ink. Scale: 2′ = 1″. Paper AF. 14¼ x 11 in. Before August 4, 1772. K33, MHi.

61. ———. General plan of top of mountain (on back of 34). Ink. Scale: 80′ = 1″. Paper AG. 9 x 14½ in. Before May, 1768. (See Kimball, "Jefferson . . . and Virginia. I," p. 117.) K34, MHi.

62. ———. "A temple for a garden." Ink. Scale: slightly less than 8′ = 1″. Paper AC. 7⅝ x 9⅞ in. About 1779-1781. Tracing from James Gibbs, *Book of Architecture* (London, 1728), Plate 67. K35, MHi.

63. ———. A garden temple. Ink. Scale: 12′ = 1″. Paper AC. 6⅝ x 6½ in. Tracing from *ibid.*, Plate 69. K36, MHi.

64. ———. A garden temple. Ink. Card. 2¼ x 3⅜ in. About 1770-1771. K37, MHi.

65. ———. Observation tower. Ink. Scale: 10′ = 1″. Paper AF. 9 x 14½ in. Probably 1771. K38, MHi.

66. ———. Observation tower. Ink. Scale: 10′ = 1″. Paper AF. 9 x 14½ in. Probably 1771. K39, MHi.

67. ———. Chinese lattice gate. Ink. Paper AN. 1771? K39a, MHi.

68. ———. Practice sheet for drawing moldings full size. Ink. Paper CX. 1775? K39b, MHi.

69. ———. "The Cornice and Capitel [sic] of the triglyph, for the lower order, External." Ink. Scale: full size. Paper AM. 21¼ x 25½ in. 1775? K40, MHi.

70. ——— (on back of 69). "The Architrave with its Tenia, and the Frize [sic] of the External Doric Entablature." Ink. Scale: full size. 1775? K41, MHi.

71. ———. "Ionic Entablature for the Upper order External." Ink. Scale: full size. Paper AM. 21¼ x 29¾ in. 1775. K42, MHi.

72. ——— (on back of 41). "Architrave and Frize of the Dining room." Ink. Scale: full size. Paper AK. 26½ x 18¾ in. 1775 or later. K43, MHi.

73. ———. "Cornice of the Dining Room." Ink. Plan, looking up. Scale: full size. Paper AL. 23½ x 19¼ in. 1775 or later. K44, MHi.

74. ——— (on back of 73). "Cornice of the Dining Room." Ink. Elevation. Scale: full size. 1775 or later. K45, MHi.

75. ———. "Ionic Entablature for the Study." Ink. Scale: full size. Paper AM. 21½ x 15 in. 1775 or later. K46, MHi.

76. ———. "Ionic Basement of Study." Ink. Scale: full size. Paper AM. 15 x 21½ in. 1775 or later. K47, MHi.

77. ———. Details of windows. Ink. Scale: full size. Paper AO. 17¾ x 14½ in. 1775? K48, MHi.

78. ———. Detail of balusters for main stair. Ink. Scale: one-third full size. Paper AP. 6½ x 12¼ in. 1775? K49, MHi.

79. ———. "[Cap of D]ado for Dining Room." Ink. Scale: full size. Paper AH. 7¾ x 12½ in. 1775 or later. K50, MHi.

80. ———. "[Base of Dado] for Dining Room." Ink. Scale: full size. Paper AH. 7¾ x 12½ in. 1775 or later. K51, MHi.

81. ———. "Drawings for Brick Molds" for chimneys. Ink. Scale: full size. Paper AG. 21 x 18 in. 1775 or later. K52, MHi.

82. ———. "Kitchen chimney" mold. Ink. Scale: full size. Paper AH. 12¾ x 15¼ in. 1775 or later. K53, MHi.

83. ———. "Base of Pedestal" for chimney. Ink. Scale: full size. Paper AH. 9¼ x 12¾ in. 1775 or later. K54, MHi.

84. ———. Detail of eaves of attic. Ink. Scale: full size. Paper AG. 17⅞ x 14⅜ in. 1775 or later. K55, MHi.

85. ———. Sketch for 75. Ink. Paper CX. About 1776. K55a, MHi.

86. ———. "South Out-house," showing poultry yards (on back: "North Out-house"). Ink. Card. About 1776-1778. K55b, MHi.

87. ———. Study for outbuildings and kitchen garden. Ink. Scale: 80′ = 1″. Paper AQ. 14 x 9¼ in. About 1776-1778. K56, MHi.

88. ——— (on back of 87). Notes for "Green house" and outbuildings. Ink. About 1776-1778. K57, MHi.

89. ———. Servants' quarters for Monticello or for Governor's Palace, Williamsburg. Ink. Paper AR. 7⅜ x 5¾ in. About 1778. K58, MHi.

90. ———. Servants' quarters for Monticello or for Governor's Palace, Williamsburg. Ink. Paper AS. 4 x 6⅜ in. About 1778. K59, MHi.

91-92. ———. Decorative outchamber with specifications on back. The elevation is notable for its fine draftsmanship, and the specifications indicate Jefferson's composite method of designing. Ink. Scale: 4′ = 1″. 6¼ x 8 in. Paper AT. Probably 1778. K62-K63, MHi. (See Nos. 5 and 6.)

93. ———. Decorative structures. Ink. Paper AQ. 7¼ x 9 in. Probably 1778. K64, MHi.

94-95. ———. Columns for "Corner temples over kitchen and servants' room." Ink. Scale: full size. Paper AQ. 9¾ x 8¾ in. 1776-1778. K65-K66, MHi.

96. ———. End portico columns. Ink. Scale: full size. Paper AQ. 14¾ x 18¾ in. 1776-1778. K67, MHi.

97-123. ———. Notebook for building. Ink. Papers AC, AN, AU, and CX. 3⅝ x 9 in. Begun 1770. K68-K94, MHi.

124. ———. Sketches for fireplaces. Ink. Paper AN. 1771? K94a, MHi.

125. ———. Lumber calculations and diagrams on the cutting of trees for the purpose of making columns. Ink. 2 pp. 12⅜ x 7½ in. Paper AD. About 1774. CSmH9389.

126. ———. Plan of an observatory for Montalto, now called Carter's Mountain. Ink. Same subject as

93. Scale: about 15′ = 1″. Paper AQ. 7¼ x 8⅞ in. 1778. CSmH9398.

127-132. ———. Surveys. Ink. Papers AU, AQ, AS. 1776-1778? K94b-K94g, MHi.

133-134. ———. Insurance plats. Ink. 8 x 9¼, 7¾ x 11 in. (134 is attached to a declaration for assurance, August 16, 1800, Mutual Assurance Company of Virginia, No. 389, Vi.) 1796, 1800. K136, MHi; K137, Vi.

135. ———. First floor plan of the remodeled and enlarged version of the house, approximately as it was built. Pencil and ink. Scale: about 10′ = 1″. Paper BD. 9 x 11½ in. 1796? K150, MHi. (See No. 15. See also 539.)

136. ———. Study for remodeling house and grounds. Pencil. Scale: about 10′ = 1″. Paper BC. 10¾ x 15¾ in. 1785-1789? K138, MHi.

137-138. ———. Studies for remodeling. Pencil. No scale, and 10′ = 1″, respectively. Paper BH. 5¼ x 3¼, 14¾ x 8¾ in. 1794-1795? K139-K140, MHi. May be early studies for Edgemont.

139-146. ———. Notebook of Jefferson's for remodeling. Ink. Paper BJ. Begun 1794? K142-K149, MHi.

147a. ———. Notes for remodeling. Ink. Paper BF. Before 1789? K149a, MHi.

147b. ———. Notes for remodeling. Ink. Paper BK. Begun November, 1796. K149b, MHi.

147c. ———. Piazza. Ink. Paper BK. 1796? K149c, MHi.

147d. ———. Curve of ribs of the dome. Ink. Paper CX. 1796? K149d, MHi.

147e. ———. "Arches in the study." Ink. Paper BL. About 1803? K149e, MHi.

147f. ———. Ornaments for dining room. Ink. Paper BL. 1803. (On back: curtains for dining room.) K149f, MHi.

147g-147i. ———. Curtains. Ink. Paper BM, BG, BN. 1803 or earlier. K149g-K149i, MHi.

147j. ———. Ornaments. Ink. Paper BO. 1804. K149j, MHi.

147k-147n. ———. Memoranda for workmen. Paper BP, CX, CW. 1804. K149k-K149n, MHi.

147o. ———. Piazza sash. Ink. Paper BQ. 1805? K149o, MHi.

147p-147s. ———. Venetian blinds. Ink. Paper BR, CX. 1805. K149p-K149s, MHi.

147t. ———. Hardware. Ink. Paper BS. 1805. K149t, MHi.

147u. ———. Work "to be done by Mr. Dinsmore." Ink. Paper BT. 1805. K149u, MHi.

147v. ———. Mantels. Ink and pencil. Paper CX. 1805. K149v, MHi.

147w. ———. Arches of passages. Ink. 4⅛ x 4⅜ in. Paper CW. 1806. K149w, MHi.

147x. ———. ". . . copper wanted." Ink. Paper CX. 1806. K149x, MHi.

147y. ———. Pedestal (on reverse: Latrobe's maize capital crowned by a sundial). Ink. Paper CX. 4 x 2¾ in. 1816? K149y, MHi.

147z. ———? "Estimate of the North Portico." Paper CW. 1823. K149z, MHi.

147aa-147cc. ———. Parapets. Ink and pencil. Paper BU, CW, CX. 1824. K149aa-K149cc, MHi.

147dd-147ff. ———. Screens and seats. Ink. Paper CW, CX. After 1801. K149dd-K149ff, MHi.

147gg. ———. Sketch of the garden, showing flowerbeds. In a letter to Anne Randolph, dated June 7, 1807. 7¾ x 9⅝ in. MHi.

147hh. ———? Drafting desk, 27 in. high, or shelves with secret drawers. Ink. Paper badly damaged. M12, MHi.

147ii. ———. Study for an outbuilding, showing kitchen, tenant's room, and lodging room. Before 1770? Paper CX. 5⅝ x 4⅝ in. MHi.

147jj. ———. Inventory of furniture, not by Jefferson. After 1826? 8 sheets, 2 double. 6½ x 7⅞ in. MHi.

147kk. ———. Inventory of furniture, not by Jefferson. 7⅛ x 5⅝ in. MHi.

147ll. ———. Miscellaneous sketches and memoranda. K149gg-K149ll, MHi.

148. ———. Window jamb, showing inside shutters. Ink and crayon. Scale: full size. Paper BH. 12 x 16 in. 1796? K157, MHi.

149. ———. Sections through passages, offices, icehouse, etc. Pencil. Scale: about 10' = 1″. Paper BD. 10 x 11½ in. 1796? K151, MHi.

150. ———. Plan of dependencies. Pencil. Scale: about 10' = 1″. Paper BD. 10¾ x 17 in. 1796? K152, MHi.

151. ———. Lodge, greenhouse, etc. Pencil. Scale: about 10' = 1″. Paper BD. 8½ x 11¼ in. 1796? K153, MHi.

152. ———. Plan of the roof and its framing. Ink and pencil. Scale: 5' = 1″. Paper BW. 10¾ x 11¾ in. Probably 1796-1799. K154, MHi.

153. ———. Icehouse, headed "plate of the offices," to James Dinsmore, March 29, 1802. Ink. Paper CX. 8 x 9⅞ in. DLC, vol. 121, p. 20,932.

154. ———. West elevation of the final version of the house as it was built; drawn and rendered by Robert Mills, who studied architecture under Jefferson. Ink and wash. Scale: 10' = 1″. 14½ x 8¼ in. 1803? K155, MHi. (See No. 14.)

155. ———. Plan and west elevation, study for remodeling. Drawn by Robert Mills. Ink and wash. Scale: 16' = 1″. 16 x 20¼ in. 1803? K156, MHi.

156. ———. Freehand sketch plan of grounds, showing orchard. Ink on laid paper, watermarked 1803. CtY.

157. ———. "Cornice of chimney of Chamber." Ink and pencil. Scale: full size. Paper BL. 10⅛ x 17 in. About 1803. K160d, MHi.

158. ———. Balustrade on top of the house. Scale: full size. Paper BX. 19¼ x 15⅝ in. 1803? MHi.

159. ———. Balustrade on top of the house, with calculations and sketches. Scale: full size. Paper BY. 1803? K160f, MHi.

160. ———. Details of cornice of fireplace? "Parlour." Ink. 11¾ x 10⅛ in. Scale: full size. Paper BY. About 1803. K160g, MHi.

161. ———. "Cornice for the door between the parlour and Dining room." Ink and pencil. Scale: full size. Paper BY. 10 x 9⅝ in. About 1803. K160h, MHi.

162. ———. "Frize and Cornice for the inner window of the Dining room." Ink and pencil. Scale: full size. Paper BY. 9⅝ x 15⅞ in. About 1803. K160i, MHi.

163. ———. "Frize, cornice and pediment for the clock." Ink and pencil. Scale: full size. Paper BY. 9⅜ x 15⅝ in. K160j, MHi.

164. ———. Pedestal. Ink. Scale: full size. Paper BY. 15¾ x 9¾ in. (Right-hand lower corner cut out.) About 1803. K160k, MHi.

165. ———. Semicircular window detail. Ink. Scale: full size. Paper BU. 17¾ x 22¾ in. About 1803. K160l, MHi.

166. ———? "Entablature for a door." Ink. Scale: full size. Paper BZ. 11⅛ x 16⅝ in. Probably 1803-1805. K160m, MHi.

167. ———? Study for parquet floor. Ink. Paper BU. 10⅞ x 11½ in. About 1803? K160n, MHi.

168. ———? Study for parquet floor. Ink. Paper CX. K160o, MHi.

169. ———? Sketches for parquets (both sides). Ink. Paper BL. About 1803? K160p, MHi.

170. ———? Sketch for a pedestal. Ink. Paper BU. About 1803? K160q, MHi.

171. ———. "General ideas for the improvement of Monticello." 14 sheets. Earliest entry dated Sept. 4, 1804. K161-K162, MHi.

172. ———. Instrument bay. Ink. Scale: 12' = 1″. Paper BS. 9¾ x 5¼ in. About 1805? K154a, MHi.

173. ———. Entablature for parlor. Ink and pencil. Scale: full size. Paper CX. 13 x 29½ in. About 1805. K158, MHi.

174. ———. Modillion for entablature of parlor. On reverse: pencil sketch for a mantel or door. Ink. Scale: full size. Paper BS. 17 x 8¼ in. About 1805. K159, MHi.

175. ———. Hall entablature. Ink. Scale: full size. Paper BS. 21¼ x 29¾ in. About 1805. K160, MHi.

176. ———. "Architrave and frize for the North Bow." On reverse: "Cornice for the North Bow." Ink and pencil. Scale: full size. Paper BS. 29⅞ x 21 in. About 1805. K160a, MHi.

177. ———. Dome room details. Ink and pencil. Scale: full size. Paper BS. 27¾ x 21¼ in. About 1805. K160b, MHi.

178. ———. Dining room arch and detail of an architrave. Ink and pencil. Scales: 4' = 1" and full size, respectively. Paper BS. 9⅛ x 10⅝ in. About 1805. K160c, MHi.

179. ———. "Drapery for the tops of 4 windows," to John Rea, March 2, 1808. Ink. Paper CW. 7⅝ x 9⅝ in. DLC, vol. 175, p. 31,069.

180. ———. Sketch for a fish pond, showing route of "pipes from the High mountain." (The pond was built in 1808 in a different location.) Ink. Paper CW. 4 x 4¾ in. Before 1808. CSmH9400.

181. ———? Garden pavilion. On reverse: plan of octagonal pavilion. Pencil. Paper CX. 7½ x 5⅞ in. K163, MHi.

182. ———. Garden pavilions in various styles, with notes. "Maison Quarree" written at top. 4 pages. Ink. Paper CX. 1807? K164, MHi.

183. ———. Tuscan monopteros, marked with the hours. On reverse: the plan. Ink. Paper CX. 6 x 6¾ in. 1804 or later. K164a, MHi.

184. ———. Notes on "A Gothic temple." Ink. Paper CC. 7¾ x 2⅝ in. 1807. K165, MHi.

185-186. ———. Plans of the North outchamber. Ink. Scale: 4' = 1" and 3' = 1". Paper BX, BY.

7¾ x 9¼, 9½ x 9¼ in. About 1803. K166-K167, MHi.

187. ———? "Measures of the roof for estimating tin: N.E. quarter beginning with the piazzo roof ... Dome. July 5, [18]22." 7⅞ x 4¾ in. Paper CW. On back: estimate for milldam. CSmH9405.

188. ———. "Architrave of the arches of the dining room," with a note regarding Mr. Dinsmore. Paper AJ. 9½ x 10½ in. During the recent restoration, Milton Grigg, the architect, found a beam with Dinsmore's name written on it. Kj, ViU.

189. ———. "Tuscan base ... for Porticos of outchambers." Ink. Full size. MHi.

190. ———. "Sketch of a column." Ink. Scale: 4' = 1". MHi.

191. ———. Plan for a nailery. Paper BK. 8 x 12⅜ in. About 1794. CSmH9380.

192. ———. Obelisk for the grave of Jefferson with his epitaph. Ink. Paper CW. 4⅞ x 7 11/16 in., framed. DLC.

193. ———. "My lands in Albemarle." Ink. Paper BF. About 1788-1793. K167a, MHi.

194-195. ———. Plats of road and fields. Ink. Paper CD, BF. October 15, 1793. K167b-K167c, MHi.

196. ———. "Field notes ... begun Sep. 27, 1793." Ink. Paper CX. K167d, MHi.

197. ———. Plan of the spring roundabout. Ink. Scale: 80' = 1". Paper AQ. 14¾ x 26½ in. Before 1794. CSmH9396.

198. ———. Field notes of surveys. Ink. Paper BL. 1800. K167g, MHi.

199-200. ———. Plats of a field. Ink. Paper BG. About 1803? K167e-K167f, MHi.

201. ———. Plot of easterly slopes. Ink, pencil, and crayon. Paper BU. About 1803. K167h, MHi.

202. ———. Survey plat of the patent in Botetourt County. Notes on interior details of the parlor and dining room. 8⅛ x 5⅛ in. Paper CX. About 1805. CSmH9369.

203. ———. Field notes. Ink. Paper CX. 1806. K167i, MHi.

204-208. ———. Plats of 1806 surveys. Ink. Paper BY. K167j-K167n, MHi.

209. ———. General plan of the estate. Ink. Paper BY. 19½ x 15½ in. K168, MHi.

210. ———. Survey of a 29-acre tract adjoining the property purchased from Benjamin Brown. Ink. Scale: 20 poles = 1". 10 x 8 in. Paper CW. CSmH9390.

211. ———. "A survey of the 4th Roundabout passing by the Thoroughfare & spring." Ink. Scale: 40 poles = 1". Paper CC. 8⅛ x 10⅛ in. About 1809. CSmH9401.

212-224. ———. Surveys and notes. Paper CE, CF. 1808-1809. K168a-K168m, MHi.

225. ———. Survey showing house, offices, and four roundabouts. The long straight line at the first roundabout indicates Mulberry Row, the plantation street. The second building on it from the right is the stone (or weaver's) house. The square at the left indicates the graveyard. Ink. Scale: 40 poles = 1". Paper CF. 16¼ x 10 in. 1809. K169, MHi. (See No. 17.)

226-238. ———. Miscellaneous surveys, consisting of incomplete studies; and some for unidentified subjects. Ink. 1808-1810? K169a-K169m. MHi.

239. NELSON COUNTY? A prison. Ink. Paper CO. 1823. (See Constance E. Thurlow and Francis L. Berkeley, Jr., *The Jefferson Papers of the University of Virginia* [Charlottesville, 1950], Nos. 2,008, 2,012, 2,015.) K215a, MHi.

240. NEW ORLEANS. "Plans of the Ciudad de Nueva Orleans, of the habitacion of Don Bertram Gravier, and of the Batture" from Carlos Tandeau. Ink (grey and blue wash added to 34,666). Various sizes. 1788, 1798. Certified by Tanesse and dated 1808. DLC, vol. 195, pp. 34,660, 34,661, 34,662, 34,663, 34,664, 34,666.

241. Map, dated New Orleans, June 23, 1805, not by Jefferson. Ink. 8½ x 11 in. DLC, vol. 228, p. 40,756.

242. NEW ORLEANS. Drawing from G. Du Jareau. Ink. 17½ x 16¾ in. August 3, 1810. DLC, vol. 191, pp. 33,899, 33,900.

243. NORFOLK. Architectural drawing in color from W. Tatham. Ink and water color. Green, slate, pink, and blue. 8 x 10 in. July 4, 1807. DLC, vol. 168, p. 29,643.

244. NEW YORK. Study for remodeling Jefferson's house. Pencil. Scale: about 10′ = 1″. Paper BB. 12 x 9 in. 1790. K121, MHi.

245. PARIS. Plan of two rooms in Jefferson's house in the Cul-de-sac Têtebout. Ink. Paper CX. 1785. K118a, MHi.

246. ———. Hôtel de Langeac. Plan for garden. Scale: 40′ = 1″. (1) Study in wash. Paper: laid, watermarked J. Honig & Zoonen. 9⅛ x 7⅛ in. On conjugate leaf: another drawing of the same. 1785-1789. (2) Replica of the second wash drawing. Ink. Paper: laid (fragment). 9⅛ x 7¼ in. 1785-1789. (See Howard C. Rice, Jr., *L'Hôtel de Langeac* [Paris and Monticello, 1947].) All CSmH9397.

247. ———. Plan for remodeling the Hôtel de Langeac. Circular room of mezzanine. Pencil on coordinate paper. 9⅛ x 11⅞ in. 1785-1789. CSmH-9376.

248. ———. Hôtel de Langeac. Study for changes. Pencil. Scale: about 10′ = 1″. Paper BB. 9¼ x 11¼ in. 1785. K118, MHi.

249. PHILADELPHIA. Details of "Governor Penn's stables." Ink. 5½ x 4½ in. Paper AS. Probably 1778. K60, MHi.

250. ———. Sketches. Ink. Paper CX. 2¾ x 8½ in. Probably 1778. K61, MHi.

251. ———. Plan of Jefferson's house on the Schuylkill? Ink and pencil. Paper CX. 5⅝ x 7¼ in. 1793? K120, MHi.

252. ———. Study for remodeling a house. Pencil. Scale: about 10′ = 1″. Paper BB. 1790. K124, MHi.

253-254. ———. Studies for remodeling Jefferson's house. Pencil. Scale: about 10′ = 1″. Paper BB. 12 x 9 in. 1790. K122-K123, MHi.

255. POPLAR FOREST. Plan of house, rooms designated in Anglo-Saxon, showing center block with octagonal projection and wings on either side with stairs in hyphens. Survey on reverse. Various papers glued together. Paper AJ and/or AQ. (See Thurlow and Berkeley, *Jefferson Papers*, No. 7.) On a photostat Fiske Kimball noted: "Plan of 1801-1806, related to early studies of Poplar Forest." ViU.

256-259. ———. Unexecuted studies. Pencil. Scale: about 10′ = 1″. Paper BD. 7⅛ x 11¼, 9 x 11¼, 11 x 8, 7¼ x 6¼ in. Before 1806, and probably before 1804. K185-K188, MHi.

260. ———. Plan. Pencil. Scale: about 10′ = 1″. Paper BD. 8 x 11¾ in. Before 1804. K193, MHi.

261. ———. Service quarters. Pencil. Scale: about 10′ = 1″. Paper BD. 8¾ x 11 in. About 1805. K196, MHi.

262-263. ———. Plan and elevation, as built. Ink and wash. Scale: about 10′ = 1″. 11½ x 9 in. (See 350 and 351, and Nos. 29 and 30.) About 1820? K194-K195, ViU.

263a. Plan of buildings for "Forrest Plantation." (In a private collection and unavailable for study.)

264. POPLAR FOREST. Kitchens. Ink. Scale: 4′ = 1″. Paper BY. 9½ x 15¾ in. About 1805. K197, MHi.

264a. Press copy of 264. Paper BU. K197a, MHi.

265. POPLAR FOREST. Roof. (In a private collection and unavailable for study.)

266. ———. Survey showing Jefferson's tract of 4,000 acres. Ink. Paper BX. 35 x 43 in. About 1800. CSmH9386.

266a. ———. Survey. (In a private collection and unavailable for study.)

267. ———. 2 items: notes on land lines of Poplar Forest; and survey of roads to Campbell Court House. (See Thurlow and Berkeley, *Jefferson Papers*, No. 1,499.) ViU.

268. Poplar Forest Papers. Surveys, plats, field notes, memoranda. 66 items. (See *ibid.*, No. 1,136.) ViU.

269. Poplar Forest Surveys and Plats. 3 items. (See *ibid.*, No. 7.) ViU.

270. RICHMOND. (1) First floor of Capitol. Ink. Scale: 10′ = 1″. 14¾ x 9¼ in. Spring and early summer, 1780. (2) Second floor of Capitol. Ink. Scale: 10′ = 1″. Paper AQ. 9 x 12 in. Spring and early summer, 1780. Both CSmH9373.

271. ———. Notes for Capitol. "Notes explicatives des plans du Capitole pour l'état de la Virginie." 9 pp. 7¼ x 4½, 6⅞ x 4⅝ in. CSmH9374.

272. ———. Capitol, as proposed by the Directors. Ink and wash. Scale: 15′ = 1″. 10¾ x 14 in. 1785. K109, MHi.

273-279. ———. Plans and elevations for the Virginia Capitol. Jefferson based his design upon the Maison Carrée at Nîmes, and was assisted by Clérisseau, a French architect and archaeologist. The plan shows a square monumental hall, two stories high, with a pedestal for Washington's statue in the center of the cella and with two large rooms at the ends. Jefferson made earlier studies, now in the Henry E. Huntington Library and Art Gallery, for a building with porticoes on both ends. Pencil. Scale: about 10′ = 1″. Paper BB, BC, CW. 8 x 12, 10½ x 17½, 15 x 10½, 12½ x 11, 14¾ x 11, 19½ x 25¾, 16½ x 10¼ in. 1785. K110-K116. MHi. (See Nos. 11, 12, and 13.)

280. ———. Original model for the Capitol, ordered in France by Jefferson and preserved in the Virginia Capitol. Scale: 5′ = 1″. 1785-1786. K117, Vi.

281. ———. Governor's House. First floor plan showing rotunda house with wings. (This may be an early version of Jefferson's design for the President's House, Washington.) Ink. Scale: 10′ = 1″. Paper AL. 19½ x 11¾ in. About 1780. ViU.

282. ———. Governor's House. Second floor plan of 281. Ink. Paper AL. 19¼ x 12 in. About 1780. ViU.

283. ———. Study for Governor's House. Ink. Scale: 16′ = 1″. Paper AX. 6 x 7⅝ in. 1780. (See Kimball, "Jefferson and the Public Buildings of Virginia. II. Richmond, 1779-1780," *Huntington Library Quarterly*, XII, 307.) K104, MHi.

284. ———. Study for Governor's House. Ink.

Scale: 10′ = 1″. Paper AW. 4 x 4¾ in. About 1780. (See *ibid.*, p. 306.) K105, MHi.

285. ———. Study for the plan of a Governor's House. Ink. Scale: 12′ = 1″. Paper AV. 27½ x 15 in. Probably 1779. K101, MHi.

286. ———. Study for plan of Governor's House similar to Robert Morris, *Select Architecture* (London, 1757), Plate 12. Ink. Scale: about 10′ = 1″. 7⅜ x 9½ in. About 1780. CSmH9375.

287. ———. Sketch plans for Halls of Justice. Ink. Paper AY. 3 x 4 in. Probably summer, 1780. K106, MHi.

288. ———. McRae House (311 N. 9th Street, now demolished). Plan. Pencil. Laid paper (envelope), no watermark. 8½ x 3 in. K198, MHi.

289. ———. McRae House. Plan. Ink. Scale: 16′ = 1″. Paper CC. 8 x 4¾ in. K199, MHi.

290. ———. McRae House. Plan and notes. Ink. Laid paper (envelope), watermarked VGA. 6 x 7¾ in. K200, MHi.

291. ———. McRae House. Plan and notes. Ink and pencil. Scale: about 10′ = 1″. Paper BD. (Plan suggests also Caskie House at Main and Fifth Streets.) 11 x 8⅝ in. K201, MHi.

292. ———. McRae House? Plan. Ink and pencil. Scale: about 10′ = 1″. Paper BD. 11½ x 5¼ in. 1809? K202, MHi.

293. ———. Plan for extending the town, the central portion of which conforms to this layout today. Ink. Scale: 250′ = 1″. Paper AW. 27¼ x 15 in. Spring of 1780 or before. (Fiske Kimball changed the date from a later one; see his "Jefferson and . . . Virginia. I," p. 304.) K102, MHi. (See No. 33.)

294. ———. Plan for Shockoe Hill. Ink. Scale: 250′ = 1″. Paper AX. 7¾ x 6⅛ in. Not later than spring of 1780. K103, MHi.

295. ———. Plan of the town, showing 28 lots from which "shall be appropriated ground for the State House, Capitol, Halls of Justice and Prison." Ink. Paper AX. 6⅛ x 7¾ in. Before July 17, 1780. Notes on back. CSmH9372.

296. SHADWELL? Study for rebuilding. Ink. Paper BI. 2½ x 6½ in. About 1800? (See also 524, 525.) K141, MHi.

297. TUFTON. Plan of the barn. Ink. Scale: about 10′ = 1″. Paper BD. About 1810-1814. K197c, MHi.

298. TUFTON and LEGO. Notes and sketches for barns. Ink and pencil. Scale: about 10′ = 1″. Paper BD. About 1810-1814. K197b, MHi.

299. UNIVERSITY OF VIRGINIA. Early study for the plan of pavilion and dormitory units. Ink and pencil. Scale: 10′ = 1″. Brown lined co-ordinate paper. 1804-1805? MHi.

300. ———. Early plan showing 7 pavilions around an open space with grass and trees, in letter to Dr. William Thornton, May 9, 1817. Ink. Laid paper, watermarked with a star above CO. 8½ x 10¼ in. ViU.

301. ———. Early studies for pavilions. Ink. Scale: about 10′ = 1″. Paper BB. 10½ x 7½ in. About 1817 or before. K207, MHi.

302. ———. Study for Pavilion III. Ink. Scale: about 10′ = 1″. Paper BD. 11½ x 17½ in. 1817. K211, MHi.

303. ———. Studies for pavilions (drawn by Dr. William Thornton). Pencil and wash. Wove paper, no watermark. 7½ x 9½ in. (Same as 352.) 1817. K212, ViU.

304. ———. Plan and elevation study (drawn by Latrobe). Ink. 7½ x 10 in. July 24, 1817. K213, MHi.

305. ———. Dormitories, West Range, with Hotels A and B. Plan. Ink. One of three variants. Scale: 40′ = 1″. Paper BD. 5¼ x 16¾ in. (See also 306, 366, 369.) 1817? K No. 1, ViU.

306. ———. Dormitories, West Range, with Hotels A and B. Plan. Ink. One of three variants. (See also 305, 366, 369.) Scale: 40′ = 1″. Paper CZ. 14¾ x 6¼ in. 1817? K No. 2, ViU.

307. ———. "Lower Story of Dorick Pavilion." Front and side elevations. Ink. "Scale: 3 I. to the

line." Paper BD. 25 x 6 in. Before October 6, 1817. K No. 3, ViU.

308. ———. An earlier study for 366, unfinished. Ink. Paper BD. 26¼ x 10½ in. Probably 1817. K No. 4, ViU.

309. ———. This is an early study for Pavilion VII, the first building erected. It shows an elevation of the pavilion with adjacent dormitories and Chinese railings, and plans of the first and second floors. On back is an early study of the Lawn showing nine identical pavilions; the specifications begin: "The walls of the Pavilion are 116 feet running measure." Ink. Paper BD. 21 x 13½ in. Scale: 10′ = 1″. 1817. K No. 5, verso is Kb. ViU. (See No. 23.)

310. ———. Elevation of pavilions with two-story dormitories (drawn by Dr. William Thornton). Ink and water color. Thin wove paper, watermarked J. WHATMAN. 13 x 9¼ in. 1817? (Edmund S. Campbell thought this might be the source of the design for Old Sweet Springs, Berkeley, West Virginia.) K No. 6, ViU.

311. ———. "Pavilion No. VII W. Doric Palladio." Elevation and three plans. Scale: 10′ = 1″. Paper BD. 10¾ x 11¾ in. Cornerstone laid October 6, 1817. K No. 19, ViU.

312. ———. General plan, sent to B. H. Latrobe from Monticello, June 12, 1817. Ink. Paper CW. 8 x 9½ in. DLC, vol. 210, p. 37,469.

313. ———. Notes on the design of a frieze: "Ionic Dentil Cornice of the Temple of Fortuna Virilis as given by Palladio and Chambray." Cornice for drawing room in Pavilion VII, " the ornaments of the Frize to be copied from Desgodets' plate 4 ps. 44 . . . to fit in an octagon angle." Paper CW. 6¾ x 10½ in. About 1817. CSmH9404.

314. ———. Survey of Lawn. Paper CX. 6 x 9¾ in. About 1817-1819. ViU.

315. ———. Detail of serpentine walls shown on No. 26. While decorative, the walls are not particularly strong. Ink. Paper CZ. 8 x 2¾ in. About 1817-1822. ViU. (See No. 28.)

316. ———. "Pavilion No. III W. Corinthian Palladio." Elevation and three plans, one with alternate

flap. Specifications on back. Scale: 10′ = 1″. Paper BD. 12 x 11½ in. 1818. (On September 30, 1821, Jefferson wrote to John H. Cocke that "Pavilions Number 3 and 7 undertaken in 1817 and 1818, Numbers 2, 4, 5, 9 finished. 17 marble caps from Italy No. 2, 3, 5, 8. No. 1, 6, 8, 10 not finished.") K No. 15, ViU.

317. ———. Planetarium. In specification book (318). Wove paper. 5 x 8 in. 1819. ViU.

318. ———. Notes and specifications. Specification book. 22 pages. Dated July 18, 1819, on cover. ViU.

319-320. ———. Study for Pavilion II (opposite sides of the same sheet). Ink. Scale: about 10′ = 1″. Paper BD. 8½ x 11¼ in. 1819. (See 321.) K209-K210, MHi.

321. ———. "Pavilion No. II. Eastern range. Ionic of Fortuna Virilis." This drawing is of an elevation and three plans; specifications are on the back. On the first floor is the large schoolroom, and on the second floor are the professor's three rooms. Paper BD. 10 x 12 in. Scale: 10′ = 1″. 1819. On June 5, 1819, Jefferson wrote that he was about to begin the drawings for the pavilions on the east. K No. 14, ViU. (See No. 24.)

322. ———. "Pavilion No. IV. Doric of Albano." Elevation and three plans. Specifications on back. Ink. Scale: 10′ = 1″. Paper BD. 8¾ x 12 in. 1819. (See 321.) K No. 16, ViU.

323. ———. Study for Pavilion VI. Ink and pencil. Scale: 10′ = 1″. Paper BB. 4⅝ x 5¼ in. 1819. (See 321.) K208, MHi.

324. ———. "No. VI. East." Elevation and three plans. Specifications on back. Ink. Scale: 10′ = 1″. Paper BD. 8½ x 11 in. 1819. (See 321.) K No. 18, ViU.

325. ———. "No. VIII. East. Corinthian. Diocletian's Baths." Elevations and 3 plans. Specifications on back. Ink. Scale: 10′ = 1″. Paper BD. 8¾ x 11½ in. 1819. (See 321.) K No. 20, ViU.

326. ———. "Pavilion No. X. East." Elevation and three plans. Specifications on back. Scale: 10′ = 1″. Paper BD. 9 x 11½ in. Alternate flap on back. 1819. (See 321.) K No. 22, ViU.

326a. ———. Same as 326, but without Franklin stoves or specifications. ViU.

327. ———. Survey of University site showing rotunda, "East Street," and "West Street." Ink. Scale: 20 poles = 1″. Paper CW. 8 x 6¼ in. (In folder with other fragments, one 3½ x 5¾ in., giving dimensions for "Perry's houses.") ViU.

327a. ———. Plat showing dates of acquisition of various parcels. Scale: 40 poles = 1″. Paper CO. 10 x 15½ in. Latest date is 1825 May 9. ViU.

328. ———. "Library." Elevation of the Rotunda. The exterior is based upon the Pantheon in Rome at one-half scale. Ink. Scale: 10′ = 1″. Paper BD. 17¼ x 8¾ in. 1819, see Kimball, *Thomas Jefferson, Architect*, p. 79; 1820, see William A. Lambeth and Warren H. Manning, *Thomas Jefferson as an Architect and a Designer of Landscapes* (Boston, 1913), pp. 43-44; 1821, see Philip A. Bruce, *History of the University of Virginia*, 5 vols. (New York, 1920-1922), I, 249. Construction began in 1823. K No. 8, ViU. (See No. 27.)

329. ———. "Library." Section of the Rotunda. Before the fire of 1895 the interior was divided into three floors, with two lower floors with suites of oval rooms, and the top floor for the dome or library room. Ink. On same sheet with 328 to its left. Scale: 10′ = 1″. K No. 9, ViU. (See No. 27.)

330. ———. The Rotunda. First floor plan. Specifications on back. Ink. Scale: 10′ = 1″. Paper CZ. 12¼ x 8¾ in. Construction began in 1823. K No. 10, ViU.

331. ———. The Rotunda. Plan of dome room. On back, specifications beginning: "Rotunda, reduced to the proportions of the Pantheon and accommodated to the purposes of a Library for the University with rooms for drawing, music, examinations and other accessory purposes." Ink. Scale: 10′ = 1″. Paper BD. 8½ x 12¼ in. Construction began in 1823. K No. 11, ViU.

332. ———. "Additional notes for the Library." On back: small framing diagram for library dome. Ink. Wove paper, watermarked S & C Wise. 7¾ x 9¾ in. K No. 12, ViU.

333. ———. Fragment of a study for the plan of the Rotunda. Ink. Paper CZ. 7½ x 10¾ in. with 2¾ x 7¾ in. portion cut out. Ki, ViU.

334. ———. Study for the plan of Pavilion VIII.

Pencil. Scale: about 10′ = 1″. Paper BD. About 1820. MHi.

335. ———. Bird's-eye view of lawns and ranges without Rotunda, in parallel perspective. Ink and wash. Heavy, cold-pressed paper. 12½ x 5¾ in. By Jefferson. Shaded by Cornelia J. Randolph? About 1820? K No. 7, ViU.

336. The "Plates, 1-15" (see 337-351 following) are not by Jefferson but probably by his granddaughter, Cornelia J. Randolph. They are inked, shaded, and tinted. Scale: about 10′ = 1″. On heavy paper, not watermarked, with co-ordinate lines drawn by hand. 9 x 11½ in. About 1820. ViU.

337. UNIVERSITY OF VIRGINIA. Pavilion VIII, elevation and one plan. "Latrobe." K Pl. 1, ViU.

338. ———. "Hotel A," elevation and one plan. K Pl. 2, ViU.

339. ———. "Hotel B," elevation and one plan. K Pl. 3, ViU.

340. ———. "Hotel C," elevation and one plan. K Pl. 4, ViU.

341. ———. "Hotel D," elevation and one plan. K Pl. 5, ViU.

342. ———. "Hotel E," elevation and one plan. K Pl. 6, ViU.

343. ———. "Hotel F," elevation and one plan. K Pl. 7, ViU.

344. ———. "Pavilion No. 1," elevation and one plan. K Pl. 8, ViU.

345. ———. "Pavilion No. 2," elevation and one plan. K Pl. 9, ViU.

346. ———. Pavilion IV. K Pl. 10, ViU.

347. ———. Pavilions I and II, second-story plans. K Pl. 11, ViU.

348. ———. Pavilion V, elevation and plan. K Pl. 12, ViU.

349. ———. Pavilion VI, elevation and plan. K Pl. 13, ViU.

350. POPLAR FOREST. First floor plan of Jefferson's retreat in Bedford County. The design was

probably based on William Kent's edition of Inigo Jones, Vol. II, Plate 17. This is one of Jefferson's most successful designs. Drawn about 1820 by Cornelia J. Randolph? K Pl. 14, ViU. (See 262-263 and No. 29.)

351. ———. Garden elevation. Regarding the ornament on the house, Jefferson wrote that he did not mind taking liberties with his own buildings, but in public buildings the rules of classical architecture should be strictly followed. Drawn about 1820 by Cornelia J. Randolph? K Pl. 15, ViU. (See 262-263 and No. 30.)

351a. BREMO. Plan. ViU. (See No. 31.)

351b. ———. Elevation. ViU. (See No. 32.)

352. UNIVERSITY OF VIRGINIA. Studies for pavilions (drawn by Dr. William Thornton). Paper CW. 7½ x 9½ in. 1817. (Same as 303.) K Pl. 16, ViU.

353. ———. Elevation of Pavilion X. Ink and wash. Thin paper, no watermark. 6¾ x 8 in. Drawn by Cornelia J. Randolph? K Pl. 17, ViU.

354. ———. South elevation of the Rotunda with south elevations of Pavilions IX and X. Ink with tinted washes. Probably drawn by Cornelia J. Randolph. Paper CW. 17½ x 11 in. About 1820? ViU.

355. ———. "No. 1. Pav. West." Specifications on back. Ink. Scale: 10′ = 1″. Paper CZ. 11¾ x 10 in. Construction finished 1822. Chimney on flap. K No. 13, ViU.

356. ———. "Pavilion No. V. W. Palladio's Ionic order, with modilions." Elevation and three plans. Specifications on back. Ink. Scale: 10′ = 1″. Paper BD. 11½ x 12¼ in. Construction finished in 1821. (See 316.) K No. 17, ViU.

357. ———. "Pavilion No. IX We. Ionic of the temple of Fortuna Virilis." Elevation and three plans. "Latrobe" in Jefferson's writing, upper right. Specifications on back. The entrance motif is a favorite of Ledoux', whose work Jefferson had admired in Paris. Building completed 1821, as Jefferson wrote on September 30 of that year. Ink. Paper BD. 11⅛ x 11⅛ in. Scale: 10′ = 1″. K No. 21, ViU. (See No. 25.)

358. ———. "C. Hotel. Ionic Dentil." Elevation and 3 plans (two stories). Ink. Paper BD. 9¼ x 12 in., with two overlays. Construction completed in 1822. K No. 23, ViU.

359. ———. "Hotel B West." Unfinished studies for plan and elevation. Paper BD. 11¾ x 9 in. Construction completed in 1822. K No. 24, ViU.

360. ———. "Hotel B. East." Elevation and two plans, with detail of arched window set in cornice. Ink. Specifications on back headed: "Hotel A. East. One story with a flat roof and Chinese parapet." Scale: 10′ = 1″. Paper CZ. 8¾ x 11½ in. Construction completed in 1822. K No. 25, ViU.

361. ———. "Hotel C. West. Proctor's." Elevation and two plans. One story. Specifications on back. Scale: 10′ = 1″. Paper BD. 8¾ x 11½ in. Construction completed in 1822. K No. 26, ViU.

362. ———. "Hotel D. East." Elevation and plan. One story. Specifications on back. Ink. Scale: 10′ = 1″. Paper BD. 10¼ x 12 in. Construction completed in 1822. K No. 27, ViU.

363. ———. "Hotel F East." Elevation and three plans. Two stories. Ink. Specifications on back. Scale: 10′ = 1″. Paper BD. 8¼ x 11½ in. Construction completed in 1822. K No. 28, ViU.

364. ———. Study. Plan of clinical amphitheatre. Ink. Paper BD. 12 x 11¾ in. Kc, ViU.

365. ———. "Anatomical Theatre." Elevation, two plans, and section. Ink. Paper BD. 11 x 12 in. Construction began in 1826. (See Bruce, U. of Va., I, 269.) K No. 29, ViU.

366. ———. Plan of Lawn with Rotunda. Ink. (306 was cut from this piece to permit substitutions; see also 305, 369.) Scale: 40′ = 1″. Paper BD. 27¼ x 12¾ in. 1823 or before. K No. 30, ViU.

367. ———. Elevation and section of Dormitories, showing colonnades and "rooflets." Ink. Paper CZ. 22 x 7¼ in. "Scale: 3 I to the line." K No. 31, ViU.

368. ———. Elevation of arcade for gymnasium. Pencil and wash. Scale: 1′ = ³⁄₁₆″. Wove paper, brown co-ordinate lines with main squares 1¾ inch on a side. 4⅜ x 16 in. Notes on reverse dated April 26, 1824. K No. 32, ViU.

369. ———. Third variant for range and gardens, showing serpentine walls. (See 305, 306, and 366.) Ink. Paper CZ. 15¾ x 6½ in. Scale: 40′ = 1″. Ka, ViU.

370. "Railing of Terrasses." Ink. Paper CX. 7¾ x 10 in. Scale: full size. Kd, ViU.

371. UNIVERSITY OF VIRGINIA. "Plan of a clock for the Rotunda." Ink. Wove paper, watermarked FELLOWS. 10 x 8 in. 1818. (ViU also has a copy made by N. P. Trist, September 27, 1827. Ink. Paper CW. 7¾ x 10 in.) Kg, ViU.

372. ———. Elevation of a Tuscan column. Ink. Scale: 2′ = 1″. Paper CZ. 5½ x 19¼ in. Kh, ViU.

373. ———. Note to Jefferson signed J. Dinsmore, regarding dimensions of the University. Paper CX. 6½ x 3½ in. Kp, ViU.

374. Elevation of three-story dormitory with eight rooms to each floor. Three floor plans. (Probably studies for University of Virginia, not by Jefferson, possibly by General John H. Cocke; see his letter of May 3, 1819, to Jefferson.) Ink and wash. Paper CW. 13 x 10 in. ViU.

375. Elevation of two-story dormitory with wings. Elevation of one-story dormitory. Two first-floor plans and one second-floor plan. Ink and wash. Paper CW. 12½ x 9 in. (Possibly another study for 374.) ViU.

376. "Plan C." Elevation and two plans of two-story dormitory. Ink and wash. Paper CW. 12 x 8¾ in. (Possibly another study for 374.) ViU.

377. Elevation and plans of dormitories. Ink. Elevation shows arches on first floor and wood columns above. "Range 589 feet. 6 inches." Paper CW. 15½ x 7¼ in. (Possibly another study for 374.) ViU.

378. UNIVERSITY OF VIRGINIA? Architrave? Fragment, badly damaged. 10¼ x 17 in. ViU.

379. ———. "Description of a joint or splice," with a cutout model. ViU.

380. ———. Study for observatory. Pencil. Scale: 10′ = 1″. Paper BD. 8¼ x 11¾ in. Kf, ViU.

381. ———. Observatory. Specifications on back. Ink. Scale: 10′ = 1″. Paper BD. 8 x 7½ in. Ke, ViU.

382. ———. Study for Peter Maverick's engraving published in 1822, showing first floor of Rotunda with oval rooms and sixteen rooms in wings, bis Library.

This drawing shows the oval rooms on the main floor, as they were before the fire of 1895. There are ten pavilions on the Lawn, one for each professor, with dormitories between them. The six pavilions in the outer wings were "hotels" or dining halls. Ink. 17 x 19½ in. (Not in Edwin M. Betts, "Ground Plans and Prints of the University of Virginia, 1822-1826," *American Philosophical Society, Proceedings*, XC [1946], 81-90.) Vi. (See No. 26.)

383. ———. Peter Maverick's plan, showing first floor of Rotunda with oval rooms, with eight rooms and colonnades in wings. 16¾ x 19½ in. Ink. Drawn by Thomas Jefferson? (Not in *ibid.*, pp. 81-89. This is another study for the Maverick engraving of 1822.) Printed as No. 26 in *Thomas Jefferson's Architectural Drawings* [1st edn.] (Boston, 1960). Vi.

384. ———. Peter Maverick's plan, with design sources for pavilions written in ink by Ellen Randolph Coolidge. Engraving. 1822. (In a private collection and unavailable for study. Tipped into Kimball, *Thomas Jefferson, Architect*, preceding Index, as a 1923 facsimile. Four copies at ViU.)

385. ———. Peter Maverick's plan, showing plan of dome room of Rotunda. Drawn by John Neilson. Wove paper, illegible watermark. Engraving, damaged. 21 x 18½ in. 1825. (For the history and various states of this and other prints, see Betts, "Ground Plans and Prints," pp. 81-90. There are eight other copies at ViU: 21 x 18¾; 21¾ x 19¼; and about 21¾ x 19 in.) ViU.

386. ———. Plan for a lecture room laboratory from Dr. Emmet. Ink. 8 5/16 x 12 in. (On verso Jefferson noted: "rec'd 12 May 1825.") DLC, vol. 235, p. 42,146.

387. WASHINGTON. Study for the Capitol. Ink. Paper BF. 7¾ x 4½ in. 1792. K132, MHi.

388. ———. Study for the Capitol, showing 4 oval rooms. (A modified scheme of this arrangement was later used for the Rotunda, University of Virginia.) 1792? Paper CX. 7¼ x 7 in. MHi.

389. ———. Tracing by Jefferson of Hallet's modifications of Thornton's design of the Capitol indicates his great interest in the buildings; it was made that he might study changes. Pencil. Paper BG. 19¾ x 16¼ in. 1796-1803. K132a, MHi. (See No. 18.)

390. ———. Plan of South wing of Capitol. Not by Jefferson. Ink and watercolor. Wove paper, watermarked Russell & Co., 1797. 14¾ x 20¾ in. About 1800. ViU.

391. ———. Sketch and notes for Capitol, "for B. H. Latrobe, Jno Lenthall." Ink. Paper CM. 1806? K180a, MHi.

392. ———. Sketch by B. H. Latrobe, showing the reason why the vault fell in the Court room in the North Wing of the Capitol, killing Mr. Lenthall. In Latrobe to Jefferson, September 23, 1808. DLC.

393. ———. Columns for the Capitol. Ink. 7⅝ x 9⅝ in. In Latrobe to Jefferson, July 18, 1815. DLC, vol. 204, pp. 36,356-36,357.

394. ———. Two drawings by B. H. Latrobe, one of a tobacco plant, the other of the capital derived from it. Ink. 7¾ x 9⅞ in. November 5, 1816. DLC, vol. 208, p. 37,148.

395. ———. Abram Faws's design for the Capitol. Ink and pencil. Scale: about 11' = 1". 18½ x 12½ in. 1792. K130, MdHi.

396. ———. Original competition plan of the President's House, Washington. Drawn by James Hoban. Ink, pencil, and wash. Scale of plan: 6' = 1"; later 7.25' = 1"; for the section, twice these figures. 21 x 28 in. 1792. K179, MHi.

397-398. ———. President's House. Pencil. Scale: about 10' = 1". Paper BD. 21 x 27½ in., 14 x 21 in. 1792. K125-K126, MHi.

399, 400, 400 *bis*, 401. ———. Design for the President's House, as submitted. Ink and wash. Scale: about 10' = 1". 15 x 16½, 8¾ x 15¾, 13¼ x 16½, 11¼ x 15 in. 1792-1793. K127-K129, MdHi.

402. ———. Study by Latrobe for dependencies of President's House (on back of 404). Pencil. 15¾ x 10¼ in. 1805. K178, MHi.

403. ———. Study for the President's House. Pencil with notes in ink. Scale: 10' = 1". Paper BE. 14½ x 11¾ in. 1792. K131, MHi.

404. ———. Sections through the colonnade and offices of the President's House. Ink. Scale: 3.72' =

1". Paper CF. 10½ x 16⅜ in. Probably 1805. K177, MHi.

405. ———. Plan of dependencies of President's House. Ink, pencil, and wash. Scale: about 10' = 1". Paper BD. 21 x 28 in. Probably 1804. K175, MHi.

406. ———. Study for section to accompany 405. Ink. Scale: about 10' = 1". Paper BD. 1⅝ x 9¾ in. Probably from 1804. K176, MHi.

407. ———. Steps for the President's House from Mr. Lenthall. Ink. 7¾ x 10 in. July 6, 1808. DLC, vol. 178, p. 31,649.

408. "President's House." Memoranda: (1) Labor for digging the Western offices. Paper CW. 3⅜ x 6½ in.; (2) Size of the rooms. Paper CX. 2 x 7 in. Both CSmH9402.

409. Study for Rotunda-plan house (probably for the President's House in Washington). Pencil, ink notes on reverse. Wove paper, probably CL, watermarked LONDON. 9½ x 8 in. 1800-1803. ViU.

410. Studies for Rotunda-plan house (probably for the President's House, Washington). Sketches in pencil both sides of sheet. Paper DB. 14¾ x 9 in. 1792 or before? ViU.

411. A Rotunda House (probably the President's House, Washington). Exercise in drawing by Robert Mills. "T. Jefferson, Archt. R. Mills, Delt. 1803." Scale: 10' = 1". 15½ x 20¾ in. (Kimball decided this was not for Shadwell: see his "Jefferson ... I," p. 119. For plan and section, see 412 and 413.) K181, MHi. (See No. 16.)

412. A Rotunda House (probably the President's House, Washington). Floor plan drawn by Robert Mills. Ink. Scale: 10' = 1". Paper CW. 11 x 8 in. 1803. ViU (lent by Graham Clark).

413. A Rotunda House (probably the President's House, Washington). "Longitudinal Section." "Thomas Jefferson, Archt Robt Mills, Del." Paper CW. 10¾ x 8 in. 1803. ViU (lent by Graham Clark).

414. WASHINGTON. Treasury office. Drawn by George Hadfield. Ink and wash. Scale: 7½' = 1". 12½ x 24½ in. 1796-1797. K180, MHi.

415. ———. Map of the future city, showing

Georgetown, Rock Creek, etc. 288 lots, some marked "President," "Capitol," etc. Ink (press copy). 15¼ x 9⅝ in. March, 1791. (See Bernard Mayo, *Jefferson Himself* [Cambridge, 1942], pp. 224-225, and Saul K. Padover, *Thomas Jefferson and the National Capitol* [Washington, 1946], facing p. 28.) DLC, vol. 62, p. 10,805.

416. ———. Drawing (press copy) showing a typical square. "The lots to be sold out in breadth of 50 feet; their depths to extend to the diagonal of the square. *Proceedings to be had under the Residence Act.*" Paper laid, watermark incomplete. 9¾ x 8 in. November 29, 1790. DLC, George Washington Papers, vol. 58, pp. 9,930-9,931.

417. ———. Method of laying out long streets (at end of four-page memorandum). Paper CY. 9 x 14½ in. November 29, 1790. DLC, George Washington Papers.

418. ———. Drawing (press copy) showing a cross-section of Pennsylvania Avenue, planted with four rows of trees. ("I think this is the best design," Jefferson to Thomas Monroe, March 21, 1803.) 9⅞ x 7⅞ in. DLC.

419. WILLIAMSBURG? "Design of a chapel: the model, the temple of Vesta. Pallad. B.4. Pl. 38. 39." Specifications on back. Ink. Paper AC. 6½ x 7½ in. About 1770. All drawings with ink hatching are generally early. CSmH9387. (See No. 9.)

420. ———. Study for plan of a rotunda house (probably a new Governor's Palace). Ink. Paper AG? 7 x 8¼ in. About 1772-1773. CSmH9664.

421. ———. "Plan for an addition to the College of William and Mary, drawn at the request of Ld Dunmore." Only the foundation for the addition was completed. Ink. Scale: 20′ = 1″. Paper AG. 9 x 13⅝ in. 1771-1772. CSmH9367. (See No. 10.)

422. ———. Measured plan of Governor's Palace, made by Jefferson to study changes. Ink. Paper CX. 7½ x 9½ in. 1768? (See Kimball, "Virginia . . . I," p. 119. Paper seems to be the same as 425; if so, it was drawn 1779-1781. K95, MHi. (See No. 8.)

423-424. ———. Studies for remodeling Governor's Palace (opposite sides, same sheet). Paper AR. 7¼ x 12¼ in. 1779-1781. K96-K97, MHi.

425. ———. Study for remodeling Governor's Palace with a temple-form roof and two pediments. Ink. Laid paper, *cardinal* watermark. 7¾ x 9½ in. 1779-1781. (Jefferson to Richard Henry Lee, January 2, 1780, is on the same paper, a fact also discovered by Marcus Whiffen, *Public Buildings of Williamsburg* [New York, 1958], p. 179, but overlooked by Kimball when he changed its date—and those of 427 and 428—from 1779 to 1772 in "Virginia . . . I," p. 120.) K98, MHi. (See No. 7.)

426. ———. Study for plan of dependencies for Governor's Palace (on back of 425). 1779-1781. K99, MHi.

427. ———. Final study for remodeling the Governor's Palace. Ink. Scale: 12′ = 1″. Paper AV. 13 x 8½ in. 1779-1781. (See 425.) K100, MHi.

428. Drawing for a bar or handle? Ink. Paper BY. About 1806? K231f, MHi.

429. "Size of timbers for a barn." Not by Jefferson. Ink. Paper CN. 1809-1810. K197d, MHi.

430. Drawing for an arch bridge. Drawn by Robert Mills? India ink. Paper CT. 8¼ x 17¾ in. 1836? K231o, MHi.

430a. Two drawings, same as 430. Paper DD. ViU.

431. Perspective view of four buildings about a quadrangle having an equestrian statue in the center. Not by Jefferson. Ink (engraving). Paper CU. 18¾ x 15½ in. K231p, MHi.

432. Template for hollow casting for vase. Pencil. Scale: full size. Paper AS. About 1778? K231i, MHi.

433. "Algerine Cement." Paper CW. 8 x 3 in. Kn, ViU.

434. Drawing of a brick chimney. Ink. Paper CW. 8⅞ x 3 3/16 in. 1797? DLC, vol. 102, p. 17,536.

435. A church with Tuscan portico. Front and side elevation. Floor plan and balcony plan. Ink and watercolor. Scale: 10′ = 1″. Paper CW. About 14 x 11 in. Design of Jefferson's drawn by Cornelia J. Randolph? About 1820? ViU.

436. Design for a desk. Paper CX. 4½ x 6 in. ViU.

437. Layout for a dial. Ink. Scale: full size. Paper CW. 1816? K231m, MHi.

438. Section of a dome. Ink. Scale: about 10′ = 1″. Paper BD. K231c, MHi.

439. Plan for an Exchange, showing a coffee-room. Ink. Paper CX. 9 x 14½ in. MHi.

440. Notes on furniture. Reading desk, cradle, bedstead, etc. Paper CX. 5½ x 2⅜ in. MHi.

441. Plan of a garden 240′ x 450′. Ink. Scale: 40′ = 1″. Paper CX. 13¾ x 21 in. K231n, MHi.

442. Geometrical drawings, probably from Thomas Paine. Unsigned. Ink. 8¼ x 10 in. DLC, vol. 155, p. 27,169.

443-444. Profiles for goblets. Pencil. Scale: full size. Paper BH. About 1794-1796? K231j-K231k, MHi.

445. A heating plant, showing pipes. On back: "fireplace" for central heating. Ink, shaded in pencil. Paper AD. (While this paper was used early, this drawing was probably made by Jefferson after his return from France in 1789.) 7½ x 12 in. DLC, vol. 233, p. 41,664.

446. Plan of house with central chimney. Notes on back. Not by Jefferson. Ink. Scale: about 8′ = 1″. Paper AA. 6 x 5½ in. 1769? K1, MHi.

447. Plan of a house with central chimney. Pencil notes on back. Not by Jefferson. Ink. Paper AB. 5 x 5 in. K2, MHi.

448. Plan of house with central chimney. Not by Jefferson. Ink and pencil. Paper CX. 7¾ x 4½ in. 1769? K3, MHi.

449-449 *bis*. Studies for a house and connected service areas. Ink. Scale: 10′ = 1″. Papers BA, AZ. 4¼ x 7½, 8¾ x 7½ in. Probably 1783-1784. K108-K108 *bis*, MHi.

450-453. Studies for urban houses. Pencil and ink. Scale: about 10′ = 1″. Paper BB. 8 x 11½, 9 x 11¾, 8¾ x 11¾, 10¼ x 16½ in. 1789-1794? K219-K222, MHi.

454. Study for an urban house. Ink. Laid paper, upper part of crown and ornate shield. 8¼ x 7 in. 1789-1790? K223, MHi.

455. Studies for a city house for Jefferson. Pencil. Scale: about 10′ = 1″. Paper BB. 11¼ x 9 in. 1789-1790? K224, MHi.

456-457. Studies for houses. Pencil. Scale: about 10′ = 1″. Paper BB. 11½ x 8¼, 11¾ x 8¾ in. 1789-1794? K225-K226, MHi.

458. Study for a city house. Pencil. Scale: about 16′ = 1″. Paper CQ. 14 x 6 in. 1789-1794? K227, MHi.

459. Studies for city houses. Pencil. Scale: about 10′ = 1″. Paper BB. 9¼ x 11¾ in. 1789-1794? K228, MHi.

460-462. Studies for a city house. Pencil. Scale: about 10′ = 1″. Paper BB. 8¾ x 11¾ in. 1789-1794? K229-K231, MHi.

463. Plan of a house? Ink. Paper CR. K231a, MHi.

464. Plan and elevation of a house, with drawings of a Chippendale chair and dormer window. About 5 x 3 in. (In a private collection and unavailable for study.)

465. Sketch for a house with a portico and dependencies. Paper DC. Probably before 1800. ViU.

466. Sketch plans of two houses and of a winnowing barn. Ink. Paper CN. 7½ x 9¾ in. About 1805-1810. K197e, MHi.

467-468. Drawings of a house for John Timberlake. Not by Jefferson. Ink and watercolor. Scale: 4′ = 1″. Paper CU. 11½ x 14¾ in. 1831. K231q-K231r MHi.

469. "Plan of a Log [outbuilding?]." Octagonal building with four rooms and a coach room in the center. Circular roof. Ink. Press copy. 7¾ x 9½ in. MHi.

470. Drawing for a metal latch. Pencil. Scale: full size? Paper BD. K231g, MHi.

471-484. Mills, canals, etc. About 1793-1817. K169n-K169aa, MHi.

485. Mills. Ink. Paper CN. 6½ x 6½ in. About 1809. DLC, vol. 194, p. 34,552.

486. Floor plan of a grist mill with detail of roller and specifications. Ink. Scale: 4′ = 1″. Paper prob-

ably AH or AD. 12¼ x 15 in., foxed. (According to Kimball, foxing occurred only with the very earliest papers which were damaged in the fire at Shadwell, February 1, 1770.) CSmH9378.

487. Map of a canal and mill. Paper CN. 7¼ x 9¾ in. About 1809 or 1810. ViU.

488. A prison with a cell for solitary confinement. Specifications on back. Scale: 10′ = 1″. Paper CZ. 4⅞ x 9⅛ in. MHi.

489. A retreat. Pencil. Paper CX. 8 x 12⅜ in. MHi.

490-491. A retreat. Pencil. Scale: about 10′ = 1″. Paper BB. 8½ x 10¾, 9 x 11½ in. 1789-1794? K217-K218, MHi.

492. A retreat. Ink. Scale: 6′ = 1″. Paper CP. 10¾ x 8 in. Paper CP. 1789-1794? K216, MHi.

493-495. A retreat. Ink and pencil. Scale: 10′ = 1″. Paper BH. 8 x 11½ in. 1794? K133-K135, MHi.

496. Octagonal building with four porticoes. A retreat? Building in form of a Greek cross, with framing plan. (Probably a development of 490.) Laid paper. 4¾ x 8¼ in. ViU. (See also 537.)

497. "A garden seat by Mr. Jones. From Chamber's Kew." Writing not by Jefferson, perhaps Cornelia J. Randolph. A study of rendering. Ink. Paper CW. 9 x 15½ in. K1, ViU.

498. Sketch for a circular stand with three shelves. Ink. Paper CX. K231d, MHi.

499. "The hewing of stone." Paper CN. Portion watermarked. 8 x 5 in. Ko, ViU.

500. Drawings for an iron strap. Ink. Paper AT. About 1778? K231h, MHi.

501. Sketches for an extension table? Pencil. Paper CS. K231e, MHi.

502. Tuscan column and base. Rendered in wash. Paper CX. 8 x 9 in. Perhaps a study by Mills to teach Cornelia J. Randolph rendering. Km, ViU.

503. Plans of two square pavilions with notes. Ink (press copy). Paper CL. K231b, MHi.

504. Working drawings for a polygraph writing machine, and for carriage spring. 3 sheets. Ink. Paper CW, CX. CSmH9395.

505. A paper protractor, homemade. Kk, ViU.

506. "Bill of scantling delivd. Mr. Fraser." Paper DC. 5½ x 6 in. Dated June, 1783. ViU.

507. Design for an urn. Ink. Scale: full size. Paper BH. About 1794-1796? K231l, MHi.

508. Fragment of a plan for a windmill. Ink. Paper AT? 6¼ x 8 in. About 1778. CSmH9399.

509. ALBEMARLE COUNTY. "Survey of 66 acres of land from Edward Carter Esq. to Nicholas Meriwether Lewis by Hudson Martin. Oct. 19, 1790." Scale: about 40 poles = 1″. Paper CX. 7½ x 9½ in. CSmH9377.

510. Survey showing the boundaries of Nicholas Lewis' land lying between Charlottesville and the Rivanna River. (Includes a town plat of Charlottesville.) Ink. Scale: 50 poles = 1″. Paper AL. 16½ x 23½ in. 1770-1775? CSmH9366.

511. Extracts copied by Mr. Jefferson from his patent for 157 acres in Botetourt County, granted by Lord Dunmore in 1774. 4 x 8 in. CSmH9368.

512. BUCK ISLAND. Survey showing two tracts of land bought by Philip Mazzei. Ink. No scale. Paper BH. 6¾ x 7¼ in. About 1795. CSmH9383.

513. ALBEMARLE COUNTY. Survey showing the boundaries of William Short's lands. Ink. Scale: 30 poles = 1″. Paper BS, with date 1794. 21¾ x 17 in. About 1796 or later. CSmH9385.

514. ———. Survey of 372 acres, 34 poles, of land for Messrs. William Carter and Benjamin Brown, by Hardin Davis, July 18, 1801. Copied by Jefferson. Ink. No scale. Paper BY. 10 x 15¾ in. About 1806. CSmH9388.

515. Sketch showing location of Lynch's patent of 41½ acres on the Rivanna River. Ink. No scale. Paper DA. 15 x 18½ in. About 1801. CSmH9392.

516. ALBEMARLE COUNTY. Survey of 496½ acres of land on Moore's Creek, surveyed for Thomas Wells, Jr., by William Woods. March 29, 1802.

Copied by Jefferson. Ink. Paper BY. 7⅞ x 9⅞ in. About 1806. CSmH9393.

517. Survey of land purchased from Nicholas Lewis (27½ acres) and Richard Overton (22½ acres). August 31, 1802. Ink. Scale: 40 poles = 1″. Paper BY. 9⅞ x 7⅞ in. About 1806. CSmH9394.

518. Survey showing the land purchased from Benjamin Brown and Thomas Wells. Ink. Paper BY. 14⅜ x 19¾ in. About 1806. CSmH665.

519. Survey showing the land purchased from Benjamin Brown and Thomas Wells. Ink. No scale. Paper BY. 9⅞ x 15½ in. About 1806. CSmH9391.

520. Survey of 1,030 acres of land on the west side of Rivanna River, one mile below Milton, by William Tompkins. June, 1812. Copied by Jefferson. Scale: 40 poles = 1″. Paper CW. 10⅜ x 15⅝ in. CSmH-9403.

521. MONTICELLO. Surveys on laying off the fields. Ink. Scale: 40 poles = 1″. 9 plats with 2 sheets of notes (11 pieces). Paper (1) BH, (2) AL, (3) BH, (4) BH, (5) AL, (6) laid, watermarked with top of coronet, (7) BH, (8) BH, (9) CX, (10) BH, (11) 8-page folder, pp. 3-6 watermarked Curteis & Sons. 1794. CSmH9379.

522. ———. Surveys of Tufton. Ink. Scale: 40 poles = 1″. 5 plats and 1 sheet of notes (6 pieces). Paper BH. 1794-1796. CSmH9381.

523. Map of the Natural Bridge (then a part of Jefferson's patent in Botetourt County). Not by Jefferson. Ink and wash. 17 x 23 in. CSmH9370.

524. Miscellaneous surveying memoranda. Ink. Various sizes. 4 sets of notes and 1 sketch (5 pieces). Sketch shows "bearing of Shadwell chimney." Paper (1) CX, (2) CX, (3) AF, (4) laid paper, watermarked 1794, (5) BY. 1794-about 1806. CSmH-9382.

525. Plat showing part of the Shadwell tract leased to E. Alexander. 8 x 9¾ in. MoHi.

526. ALBEMARLE COUNTY. Surveys and plats of Monticello, Edgehill, Shadwell, Pantops and Lego. 7 items, undated. FC3135, FC3136, FC3137, FC3138, FC3142, FC3143, ViU.

527. ANNAPOLIS. Hammond-Harwood house, meas-

ured drawings of the plan and elevation showing windows and door. Ink. Paper AZ. 7¼ x 8¾ in. 1783-1784. MHi.

528. MONTICELLO. Survey showing oval boundary of the northeast lawn. Ink. Scale: 20′ = 1″. Paper BR. 10 x 15½ in. After 1803. MHi.

529. A retreat. A study for 493. Pencil. 7⅞ x 12¼ in. 1794? MHi.

530. Barn and shed. Specifications, with sketch of barn. Ink. 4⅞ x 8¼ in. MHi.

531. Combined writing desk and dressing table. Ink. 15 x 8½ in. MHi.

532. Drawings for a carriage. Ink. Five "figs" and notes on three sheets. Ca. 1805-1806. FC2713, ViU.

533. Sketches for the body of a carriage. M1, M2, MHi.

534. Sketch for body and frame of a carriage, with notes. Press copy. M11, MHi.

535. Sketches of "Clarke's Jaunting car." M13, MHi.

536. CUMBERLAND COUNTY. Map copied from one prepared by George Carrington. Dated 1777 May 2. FC2353, ViU.

537. Rough plan of porticoed building with four octagonal rooms arranged about a square. On verso of letter, 1777 August 15 from Charles S. Lewis, Jr. May be related to 496. ViU 9828a.

538. Sketch for a table, ca. 1782. FC2382, ViU.

539. MONTICELLO. Preliminary plan for east front addition. [Ante 1794]. ViU 9090a. (See also 135.)

540. ———. Notes for construction of icehouse, coachrooms, etc. M3, MHi.

541. Sketch and specifications for spectacles, ca. 1789. FC2432, ViU.

542. ALBEMARLE COUNTY. Survey map of road from Secretary's Ford. Dated April 16, 1794. FC-2534, ViU.

543. ———. Survey of Lego. Dated July 29, 1794. FC2536, ViU.

544. ———. Surveys of [Monticello]. One dated 1795 June 16. Three items. FC2540, ViU.

545. BEDFORD COUNTY. Plat of land of T. M. Randolph and others. [Post 1800]. Scale: 100 poles = 1″. ViU 9090a.

546. ALBEMARLE COUNTY. Survey of Monticello, with outline of buildings. Dated 1806 August 3. FC2720, ViU.

547. ———. Plat of Lego. Press copy. Dated December 29, 1809. FC2789, ViU.

548. ———. Survey of line between Lego and Pantops. Dated 1811 April 17. FC2801, ViU.

549. ———. Plat of lands of Charles Lewis Bankhead. Dated 1811 April. ViU 1397.

550. CAMPBELL COUNTY. Copies of exhibits in answer to suit of Scott v. Jefferson and Harrison. Ca. 1812 August. TB1188, ViU.

551. Drawing [for the base of a globe]. M23, MHi.

552. Drawings for delineations of the path of the sun (for use with a globe?). Not by Jefferson. M20, M25, MHi.

553. Trigonometric calculations for arcs of two domes or globes. On verso of letter, 1819 April 9 from Edmund Bacon. FC2951, ViU.

554. UNIVERSITY OF VIRGINIA. Three plats of University land, ca. 1819. TB1761, ViU. (See also 327a.)

555. ———. "Instructions to Mr. Brockenbrough" concerning construction of university buildings and water supply system, including a sketch for measuring "the typanum of the portico of the Rotunda" for a clock and bell. TB2324, ViU.

556. Sketch and specifications for a game bag. TB2337, ViU.

557. ALBEMARLE COUNTY. Map of area from Charlottesville to Milton. FC3131, ViU.

558. ———. Plat of Harrison family land. FC3132, ViU.

559. VIRGINIA. Map of James River and Fluvanna River basins from Richmond to Monticello. FC3133, ViU.

560. ALBEMARLE COUNTY. Plat of land of Nicholas M. Lewis. FC3134, ViU.

561. Drawing for a locking mechanism(?). ViU 5533.

562. MONTICELLO. Rough sketch of outline of house and dependencies. Authenticated in unidentified hand. ViU 9828.

563. ————. Two sketches of plan showing locations of furnishings and works of art. By Cornelia J. Randolph. Post July, 1826. ViU.

564. Notes on "Horse Wheels" for mills at Tufton and Lego. Calculations on verso are by Jefferson. FC3109, ViU.

565. Drawings for a "Horse Wheel" [threshing machine]. Not by Jefferson. M7, M8, MHi.

566. Sketches and specifications for a wind vane [to operate machinery?]. Badly damaged. M16, M17, MHi.

567. Sketches for machines for milling flour, "for working fire engine" and "for breaking plaister." M6, MHi.

568. Cross-sectional drawing [for construction of a beam]. M5, MHi.

569. Drawing for a book press or cabinet. M26, MHi.

570. Sketch and specifications for a book press with drawer. MHi.

571. Rough sketch for a fireplace. M19, MHi.

572. Sketches for bolt heads (?) to be cast in iron. M21, MHi.

573. Sketches of an apple press. MHi.

574. Sketch of Paul Pilsbury's machine for shelling Indian corn. DLC.

575. "A Portable copying press." Drawings and specifications. M18, MHi.

576. Sketches and notes for a "Portable Frame for [constructing] Ridges." Fragment. FC3107, ViU.

Index to Papers Used by Jefferson

AA. Laid paper. Watermark: Ornate shield with coronet above. Incomplete below.

AB. Laid paper. Watermarks: (1) A circle enclosing a crown with G R below and leafage at the sides. (2) Arms of England with crown sunk in the ribbon.

AC. Laid paper. Watermarks: (1) Crown, G R below. (2) Arms of England with crown above. [Used in 1768, 1769, and 1770.]

AD. Laid paper. Watermark: Arms of England with crown above.

AE. Laid paper. Watermark: Posthorn in ornate shield. Coronet above. Incomplete below.

AF. Laid paper. Watermark: Posthorn, with bell at left, in ornate shield. Coronet above, G R below.

AG. Laid paper. Watermarks: (Left) IV. (Right) Posthorn, with bell at left, in ornate shield. Coronet above, bell below, hanging from shield.

AH. Laid paper. Watermark: A Crown with G R below.

AI. Laid paper. Watermark: A circle, having within, at the top, a crown, flanked by leafage. Lower half of circle missing.

AJ. Laid paper. Watermark: J. WHATMAN.

AK. Laid paper. Watermarks: (Left) J WHATMAN. (Right) Fleur-de-lis in ornate shield. Coronet above, G R below.

AL. Laid paper. Watermarks: (Left) W. (Right) Shield with a bendlet. Fleur-de-lis above, L V G[ERREVINK] below.

AM. Laid paper. Watermarks: (Left) IV. (Right) Ornate shield enclosing a fleur-de-lis with small T in center lobe. Above, a coronet, below, a 4, with L V G[ERREVINK] below it.

AN. Laid paper. Watermark: Posthorn in ornate shield. Incomplete above, L V G[ERREVINK] below.

AO. Laid paper. Watermarks: (Left) IV. (Right) Posthorn with bell at left, in ornate shield. Coronet above, L V G[ERREVINK] below.

AP. Laid paper. Watermark: An interlace enclosed in a circle.

AQ. Laid paper. Watermarks: (Left) J WHATMAN & Co. (Right) Posthorn, with bell at right, in ornate shield. Coronet above, G R below.

AR. Bluish laid paper. No watermark.

AS. Laid paper. Watermarks: (Left) Britannia with a lion rampant surrounded by a palisade. Motto: PRO PATRIA. (Right) Crown, lower portion incomplete.

AT. Laid paper. Watermark: On a shield within a wreath, a griffin (?) segreant, on a chief three fleurs-de-lis.

AU. Laid paper. Watermarks: (Left) Circle enclosing an inverted bell with G R below it and surrounded by leafage. (Right) Britannia within a ribbon, with crown above.

AU *bis.* Laid paper. Watermark: Britannia within a ribbon. Crown above.

AV. Very thick yellowish laid paper with small fragment of watermark of a nature not determinable.

AW. Laid paper. Watermarks: (Left) IV. (Right) Posthorn, with bell at right, in ornate shield, coronet above. L V GERREVINK below. Small W in center of the sheet.

AX. Laid paper. Watermark: Sceptre terminating in a fleur-de-lis.

AY. Laid paper. Watermark: Crown. Incomplete.

AZ. Laid paper. Watermark: TAYLOR.

BA. Laid paper. Watermark: coronet and ornate shield. Incomplete.

BB. Wove paper. No watermark. Engraved with co-ordinate lines in red ink, every tenth line emphasized. These main divisions are slightly less than the English inch, by an amount varying from $\frac{3}{16}$″ to $\frac{3}{8}$″ less in the total length of the plate, about twelve and a half inches. This shortage conforms to what might be expected from the shrinkage of the paper after impression, so that the divisions were doubtless intended for English inches and tenths.

BC. Wove paper. No watermark. Embossed with co-ordinate lines spaced ten to the English inch.

BD. Laid paper. Watermarks: (I) I H S in a circle. (II, upside down in relation to I) Moyen de J ❀ Berger. Engraved with fine co-ordinate lines in brown ink, every tenth line emphasized. English inches and tenths, less shrinkage.

BE. Laid paper. Watermark: VAN DER LEY.

BF. Laid paper. Watermarks: (Left) S & C.

(Right) Posthorn, with bell at right, in ornate shield. Coronet above, L V G below.

BG. Laid paper. Watermark: Posthorn, with bell at left, in ornate shield. Coronet above, script C & S below.

BH. Laid paper. Watermarks: (Left) D. & C. BLAUW. (Right) Lion rampant gardant on a book (?) with the inscription URYHEYT. In the dexter paw a sheaf of arrows, in the sinister paw a cresset (?). The whole within a ribbon bearing the motto "PRO PATRIA EIUSQUE LIBERTATE," and surmounted by an imperial crown. Below, B.

BI. Wove paper. Watermark: BUDGEN; below, 1797.

BJ. Wove paper. Watermark: COURIALIN.

BK. Laid paper. Watermarks: (I) J LARKING. (II) Posthorn, with bell at left, in ornate shield. Coronet above, G R below.

BL. Laid paper. Watermark: Posthorn in ornate shield. Coronet above, flourished W below.

BM. Laid paper. Watermark: L MUNN; beneath, 1794.

BN. Laid paper. Watermark: CURTEIS & SONS; below, 1799.

BO. Laid paper. Watermark: Arms of Great Britain within a ribbon. Crown above.

BP. Wove paper. Watermark: J RUSE; below, 1801.

BQ. Wove paper. Watermark: 1801.

BR. Laid paper. Watermark: 1803.

BS. Laid paper. Watermarks: (Left) J WHATMAN. (Right) Fleur-de-lis in ornate shield. Coronet above, flourished W below.

BT. Wove paper. Watermark: J LARKING.

BU. Wove paper. Watermark: W.

BV. Laid paper. Watermark: Britannia within a ribbon. Crown above. Fragment only.

BW. Laid paper. Watermark: On a shield, surmounted by a fleur-de-lis, a bendlet, below a monogram (incomplete).

BX. Laid paper. Watermarks: (Left) M B, 1799 below. (Right) Posthorn, with bell at left, in ornate shield. Crown above, 1799 below.

BY. Laid paper. Watermarks: (Left) AUSTIN. (Right) Fleur-de-lis, 1800 below.

BZ. Wove paper. Watermark: T G & Co.

CA. Wove paper. Watermarks: (I) MAGNAY & PICKERING. (2) LONDON.

CB. Laid paper. Watermarks: (Left) Lower part of some letters, indistinguishable. (Right) Lower part of a device, indistinguishable. Script "hollande" below.

CC. Laid paper. Watermark: H & P.

CD. Laid paper. Watermarks: (Left) . . . ONS. (Right) Incomplete. A crown at top.

CE. Laid paper. Watermark: Incomplete. Posthorn in ornate shield. Crown (?) above.

CF. Laid paper. Watermarks: (Left) 1803. (Right) Posthorn, with bell at right, in ornate shield. Coronet above, flourished W below. Small circle in the center of the sheet.

CG. Laid paper. Watermarks: (Left) RADWAY, 1802 below. (Right) On a shield, quarterly, surmounted by a crown: first, three lions passant gardant; second, a lion (?) rampant; third, a harp; fourth, a horse, courant.

CH. Laid paper. Watermark: J WHATMAN.

CI. Laid paper. Watermark: 1796.

CJ. Laid paper. Watermark: A bell, with script T W in a band across it.

CK. Wove paper. Watermark: AMIES.

CL. Wove paper. Watermark: J WATT & Co PATent COPYING | Sold by J WOOD MASON | LONDON.

CM. Wove paper. Watermark: Eagle with United States shield.

CN. Wove paper. Letters of Aug. 24, 1809, Aug. 2, 1810. MHi. Watermark: A bird with a twig in its bill.

CO. Wove paper. Watermark: D AMES.

CP. Laid paper. Watermark: Britannia within a ribbon. Crown above, script AB below.

CQ. Wove paper. Engraved with co-ordinate lines in red ink, every tenth line emphasized. Sixteenths of the English inch, less shrinkage. Engraved on margin: "A Paris chez Crepy rue S. Jacques à S. Pierre pres la rue de la parcheminerie. du 10 en 10."

CR. Laid paper. Watermark: Incomplete. Portion of an ornate shield with coronet above.

CS. Laid paper. Watermark: Incomplete. SAND . . .

CT. Wove paper. Watermark: P H & S.

CU. Wove paper. Watermark: J WHATMAN, below, 1801.

CV. Wove paper. Watermark: EHRHART.

CW. Wove paper, no watermark.

CX. Laid paper, no watermark.

CY. Laid paper. Watermark: J BIGG.

CZ. Laid paper. No watermarks. Co-ordinate paper engraved in brown ink, etc.

DA. Laid paper. Watermark: (Left) W. STIDOLPH. (Right) Posthorn in ornate shield. Coronet above, G R below.

DB. Laid paper. Watermark: Posthorn in ornate shield, coronet above, bell below, TAR KOOL.

DC. Laid paper. Watermark: A crown, incomplete below.

DD. Wove paper. Watermark: J WHATMAN TURKEY MILL 1836.